ADULT COLORING BOOK

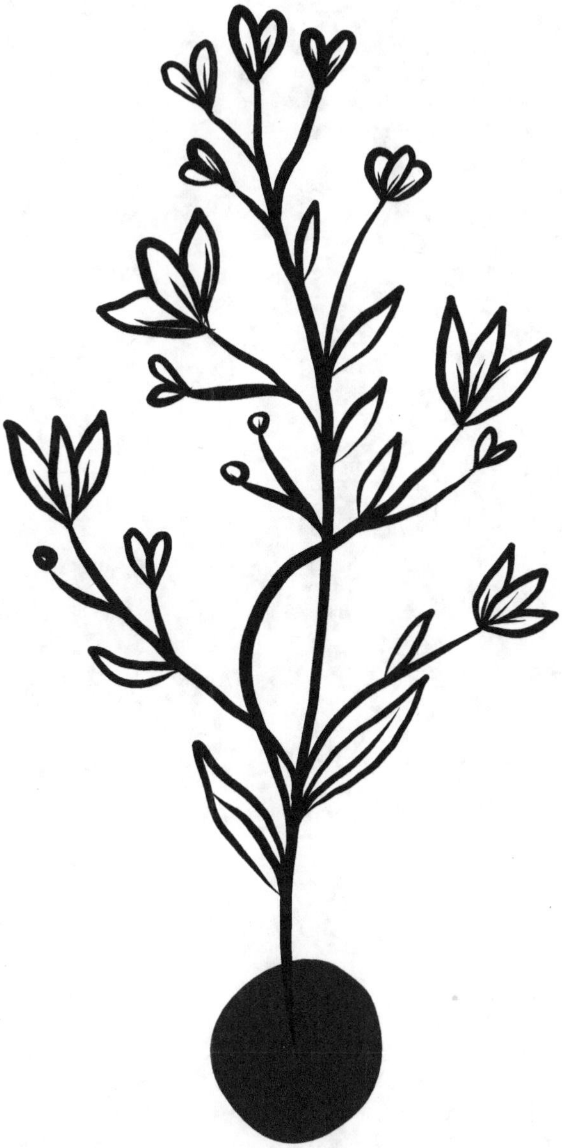

GOBLIN

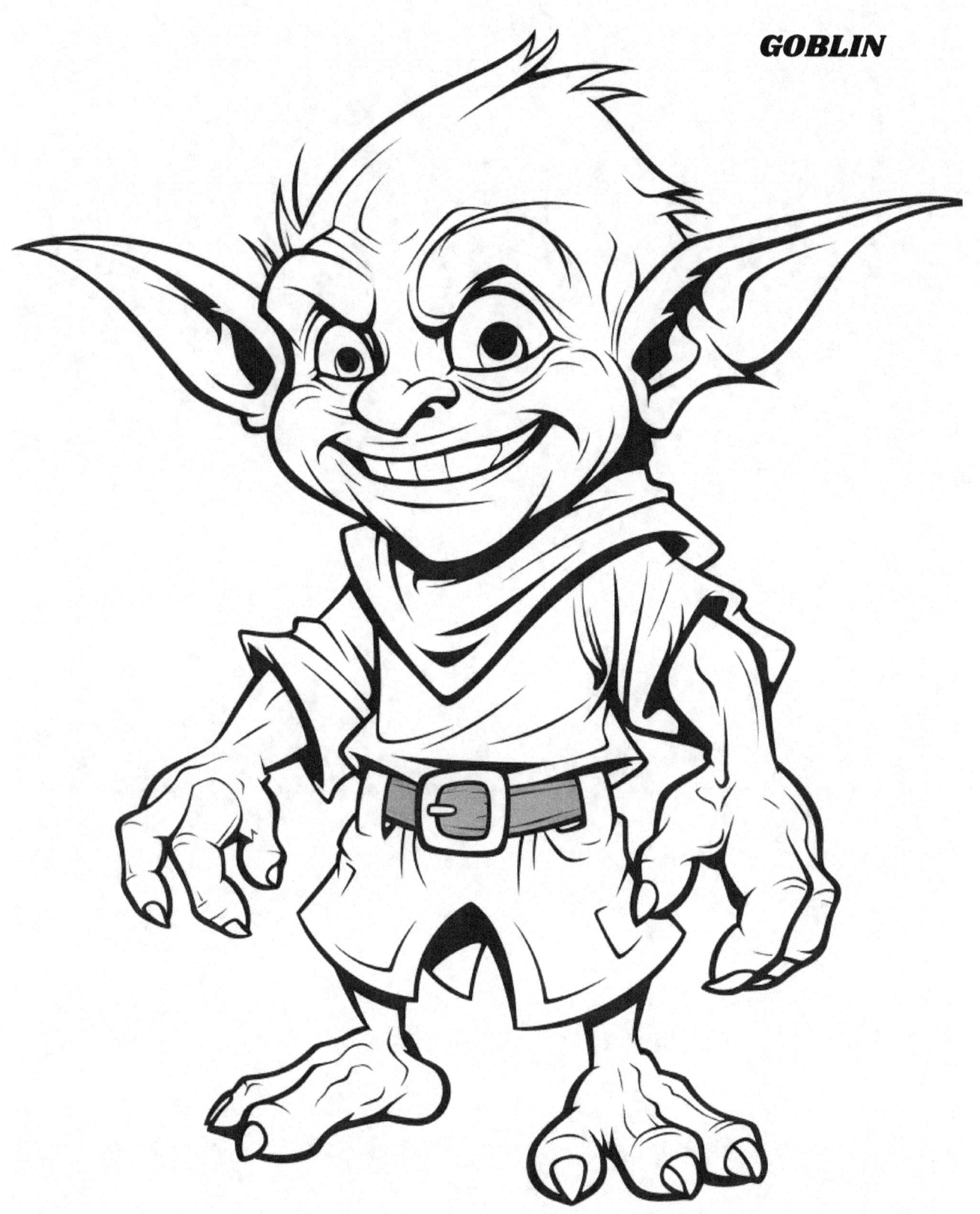

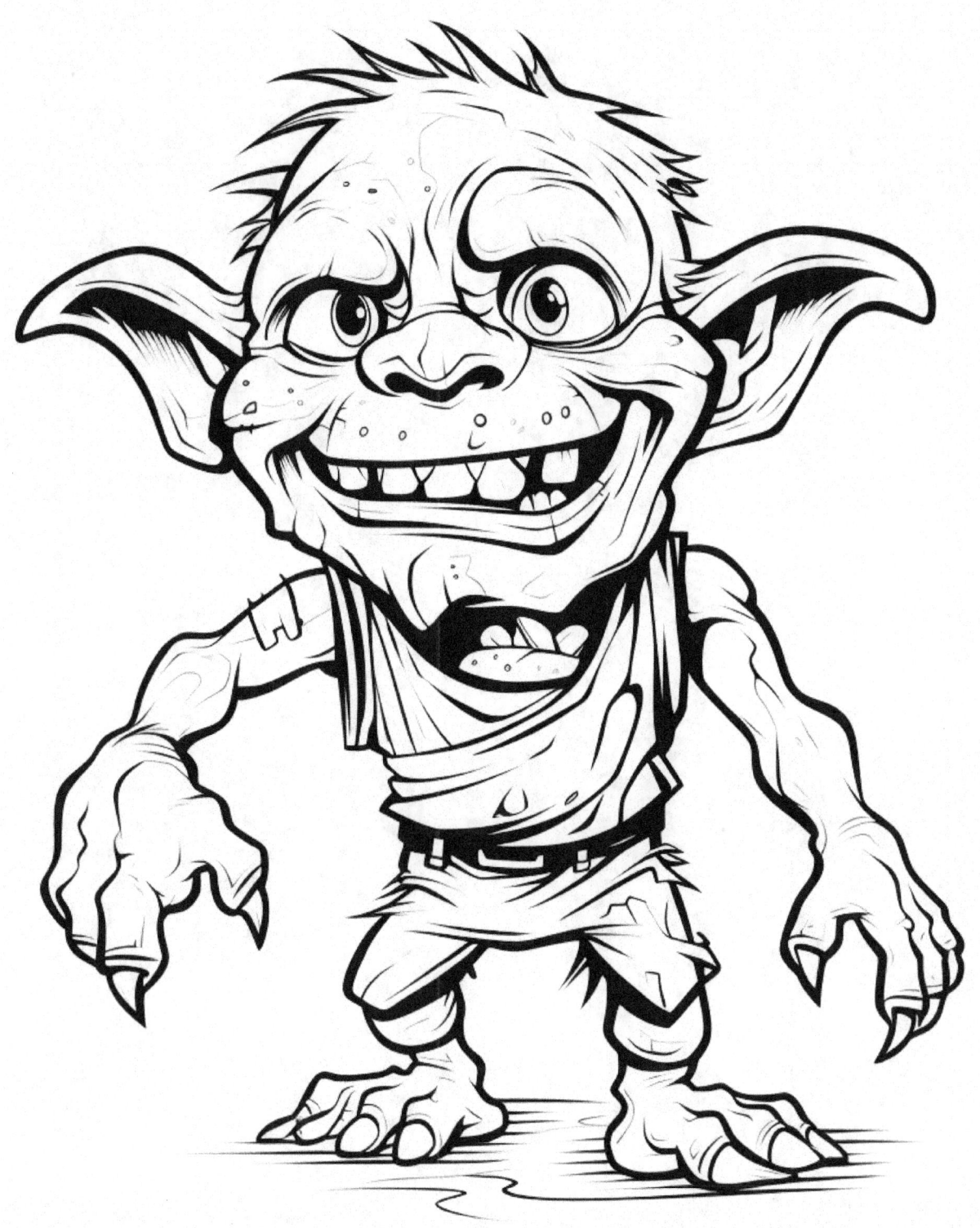

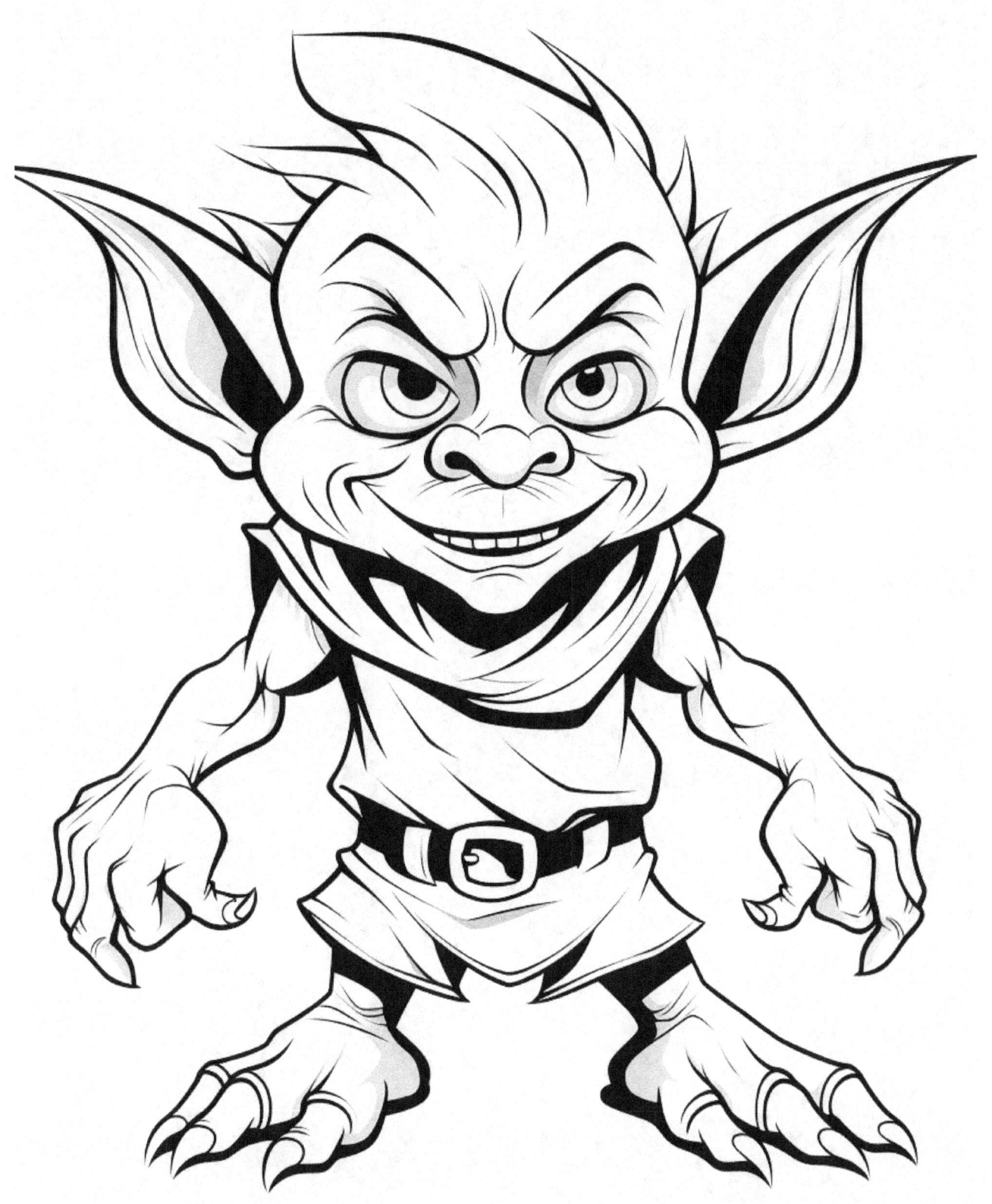

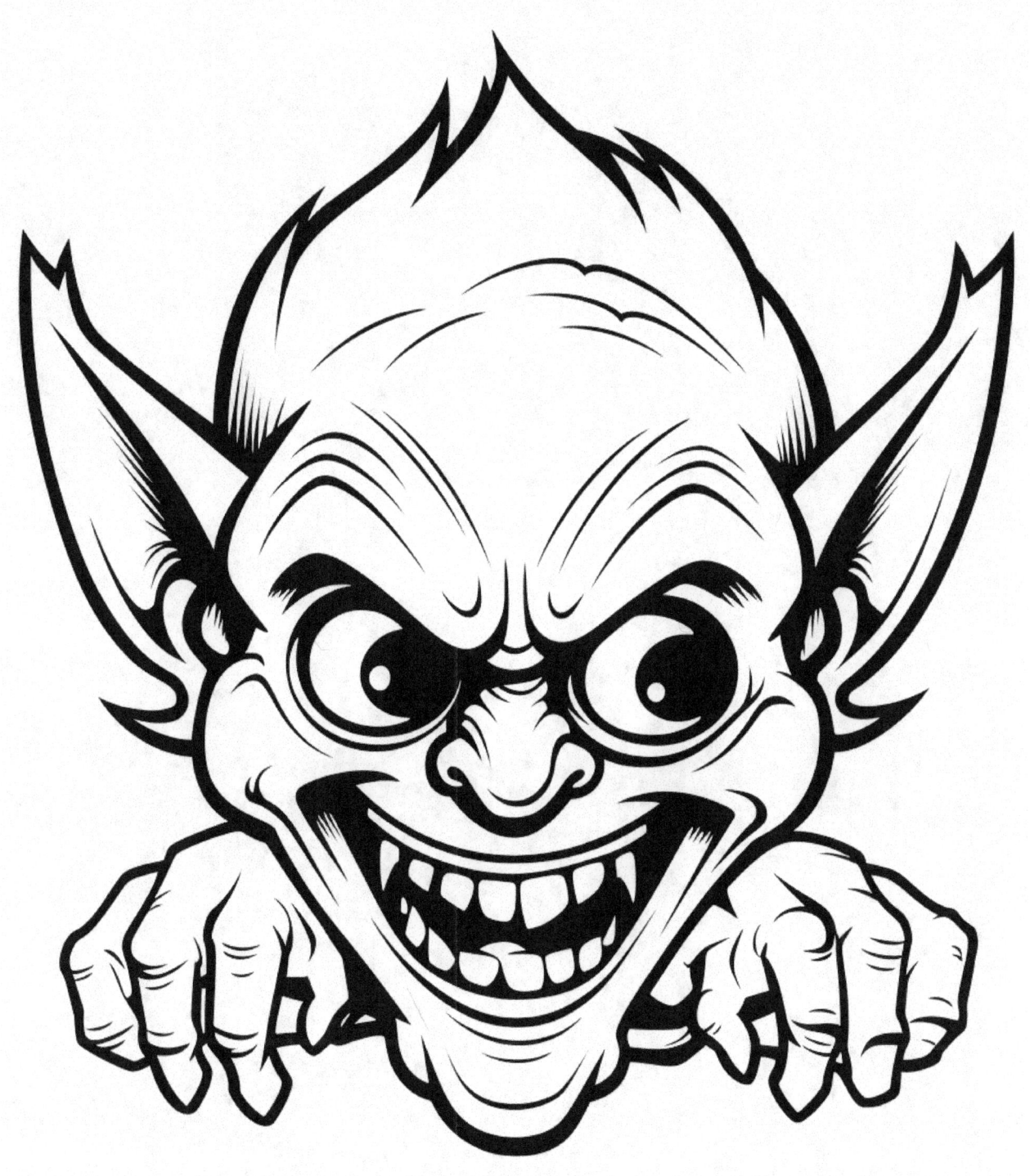

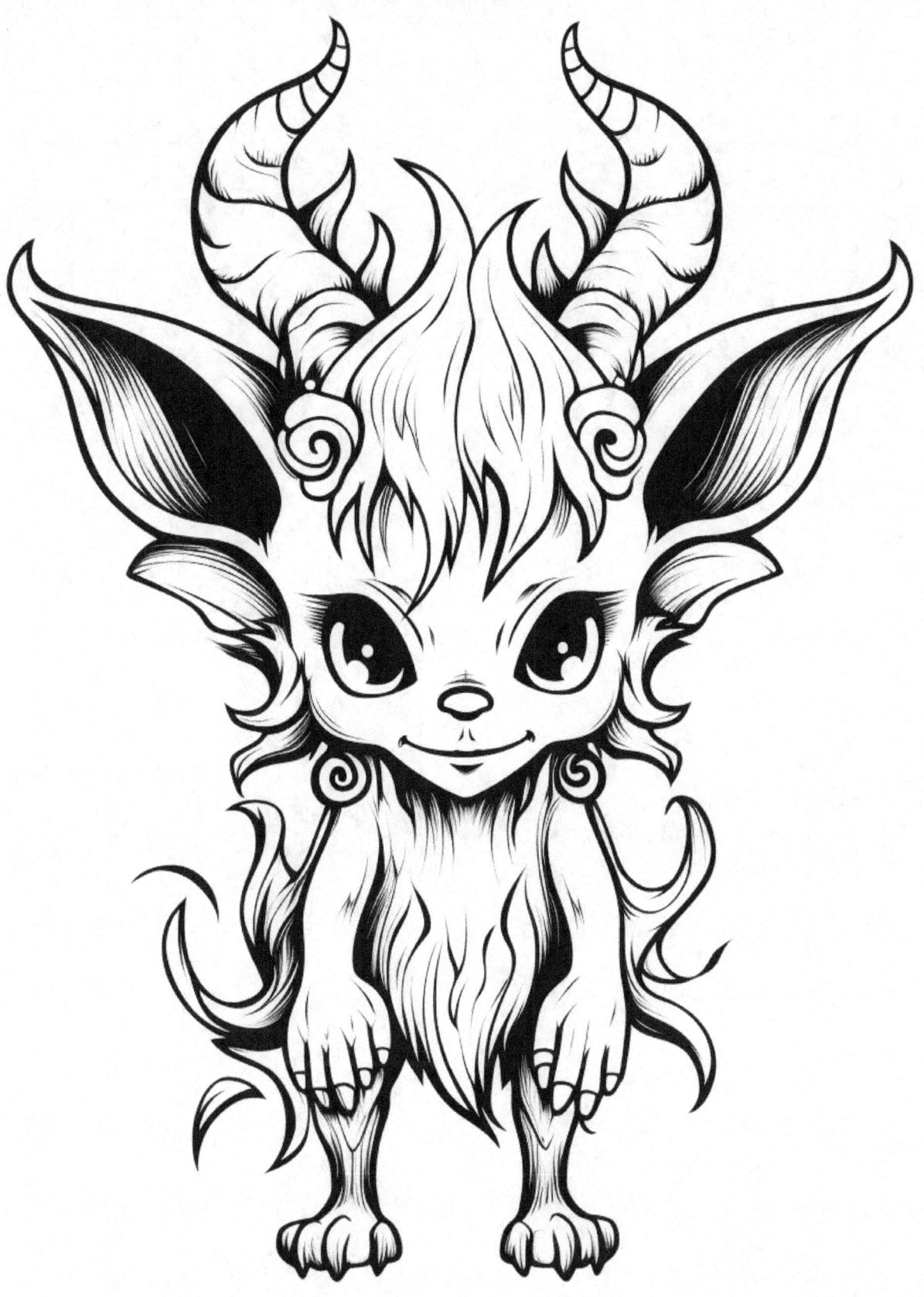

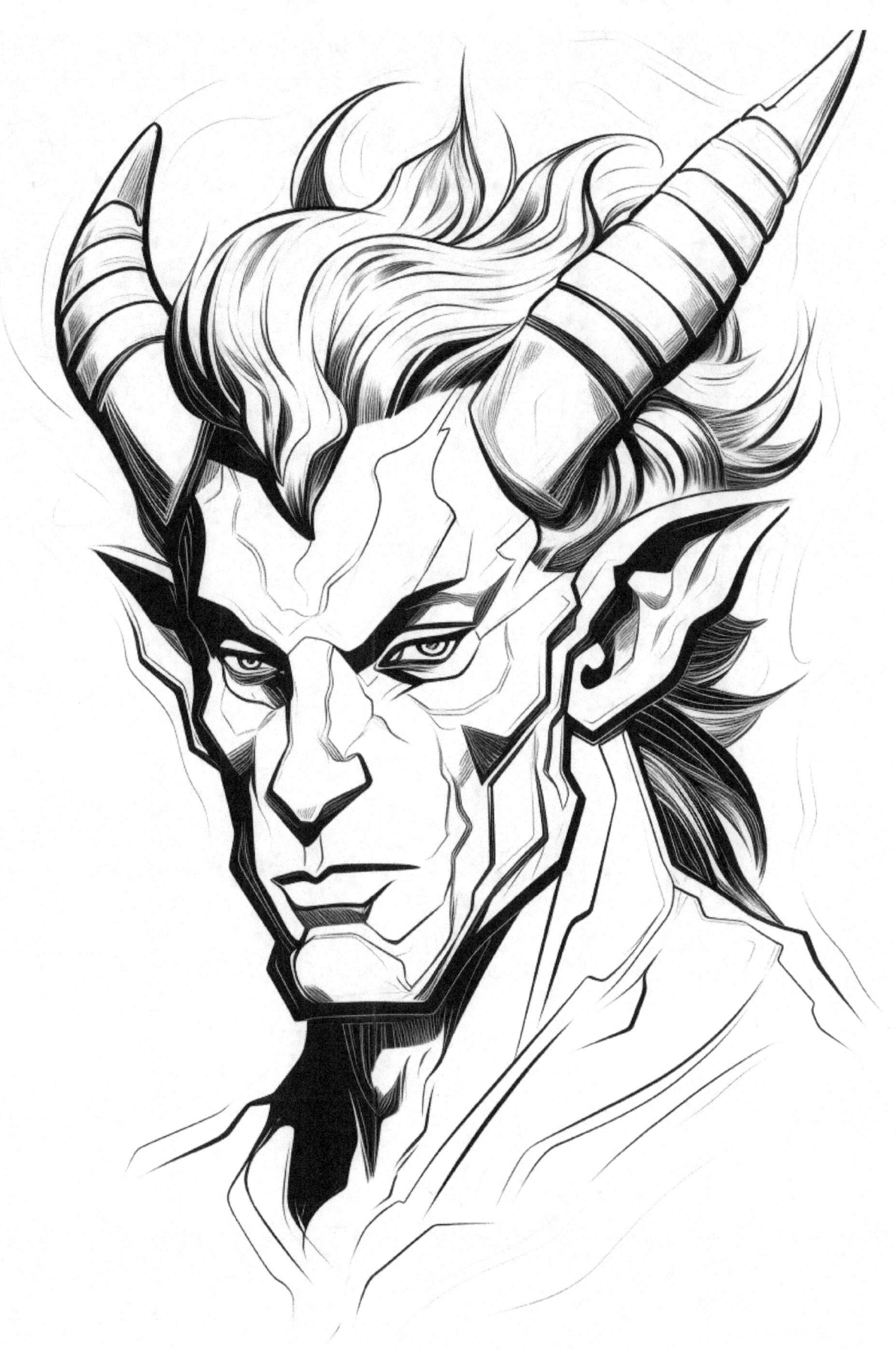

BANSHEE

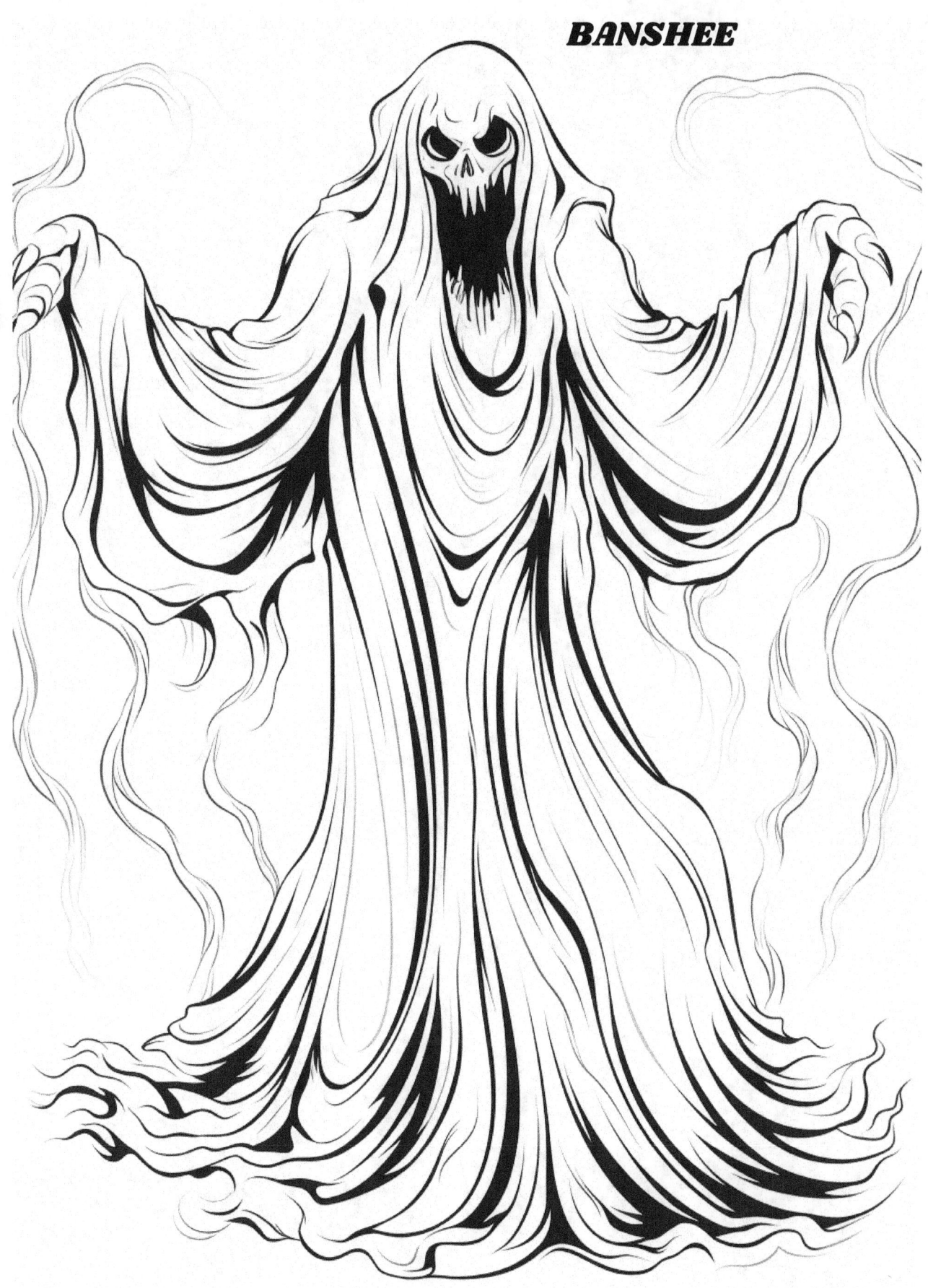

MINOTAUR

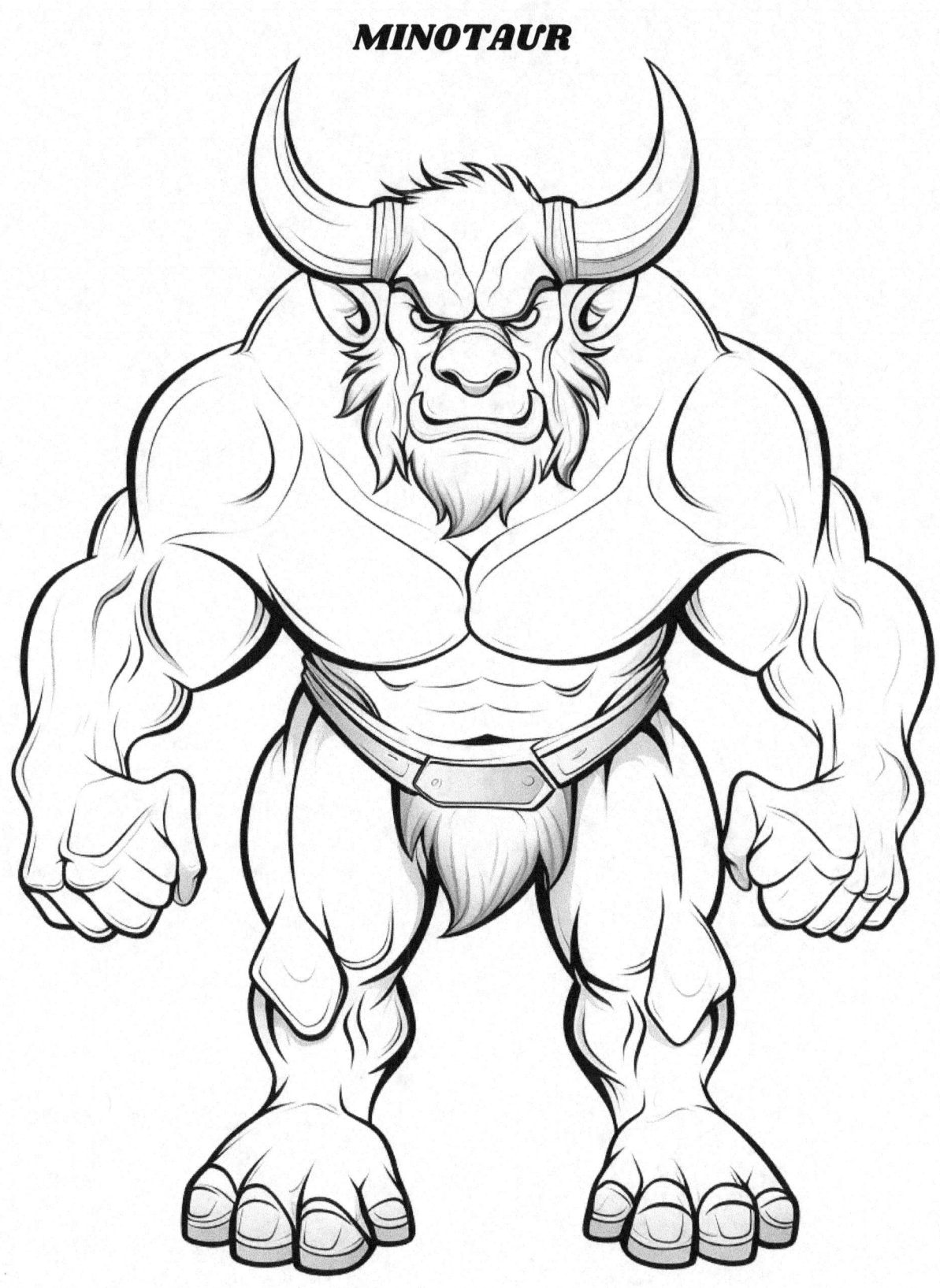

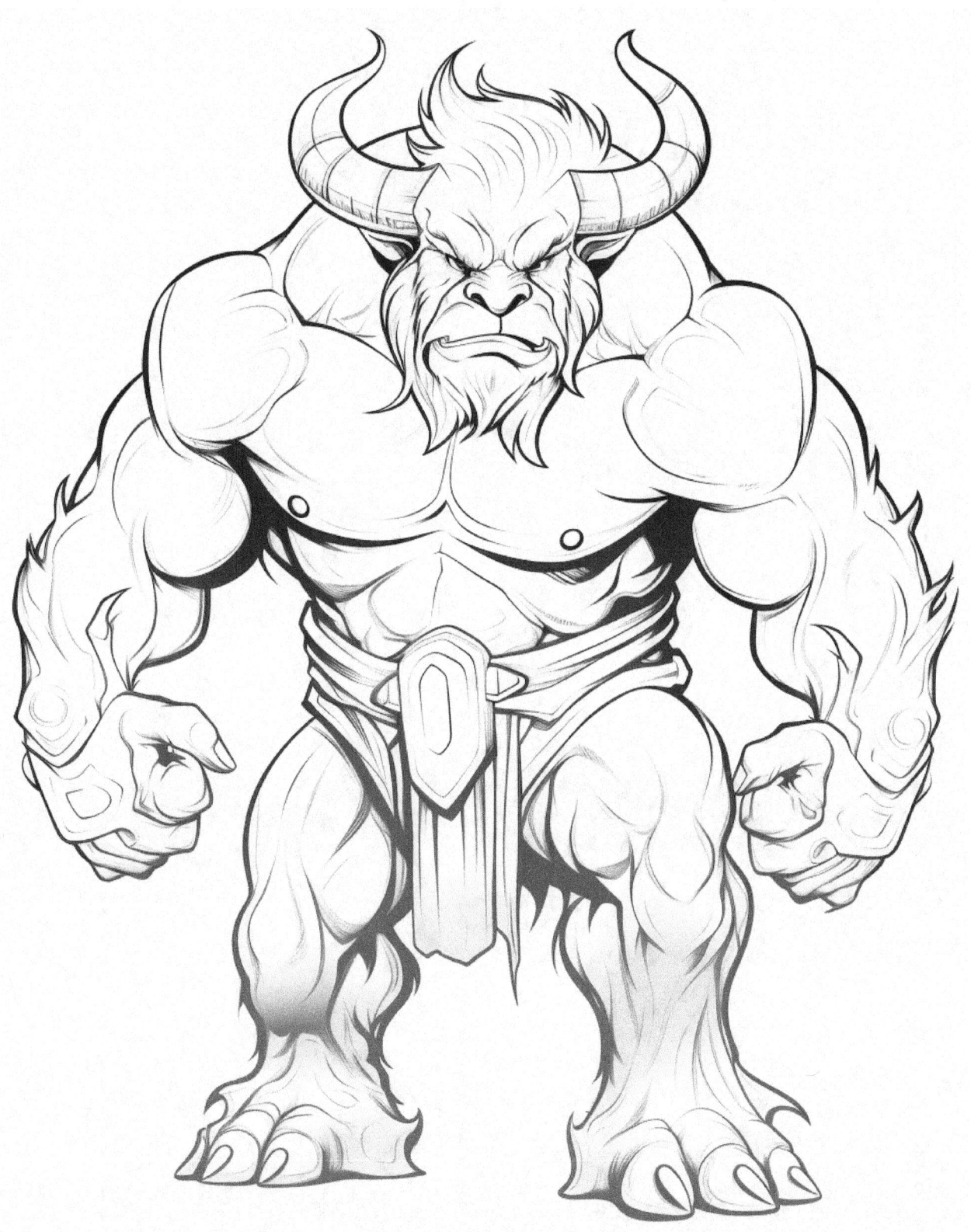

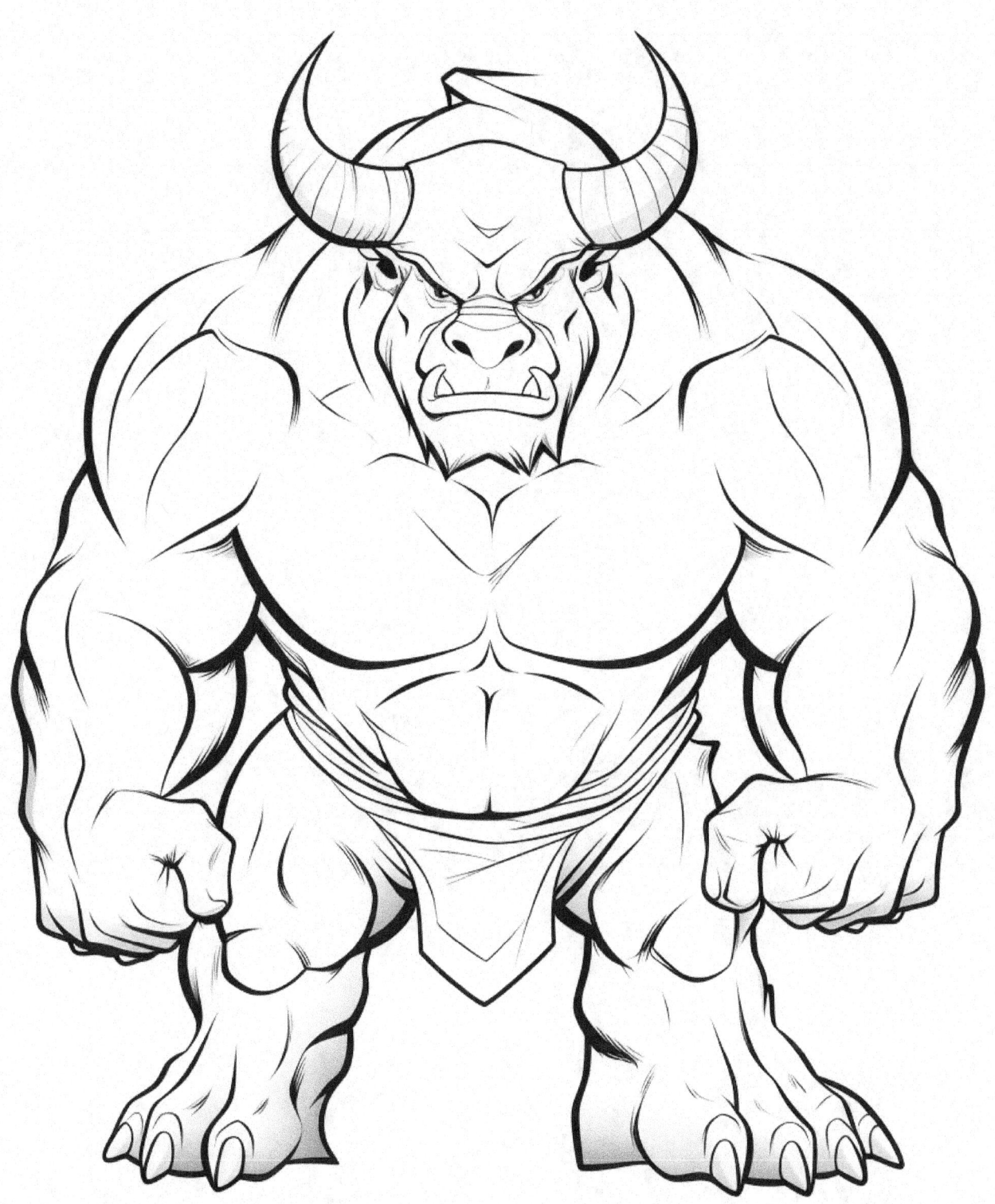

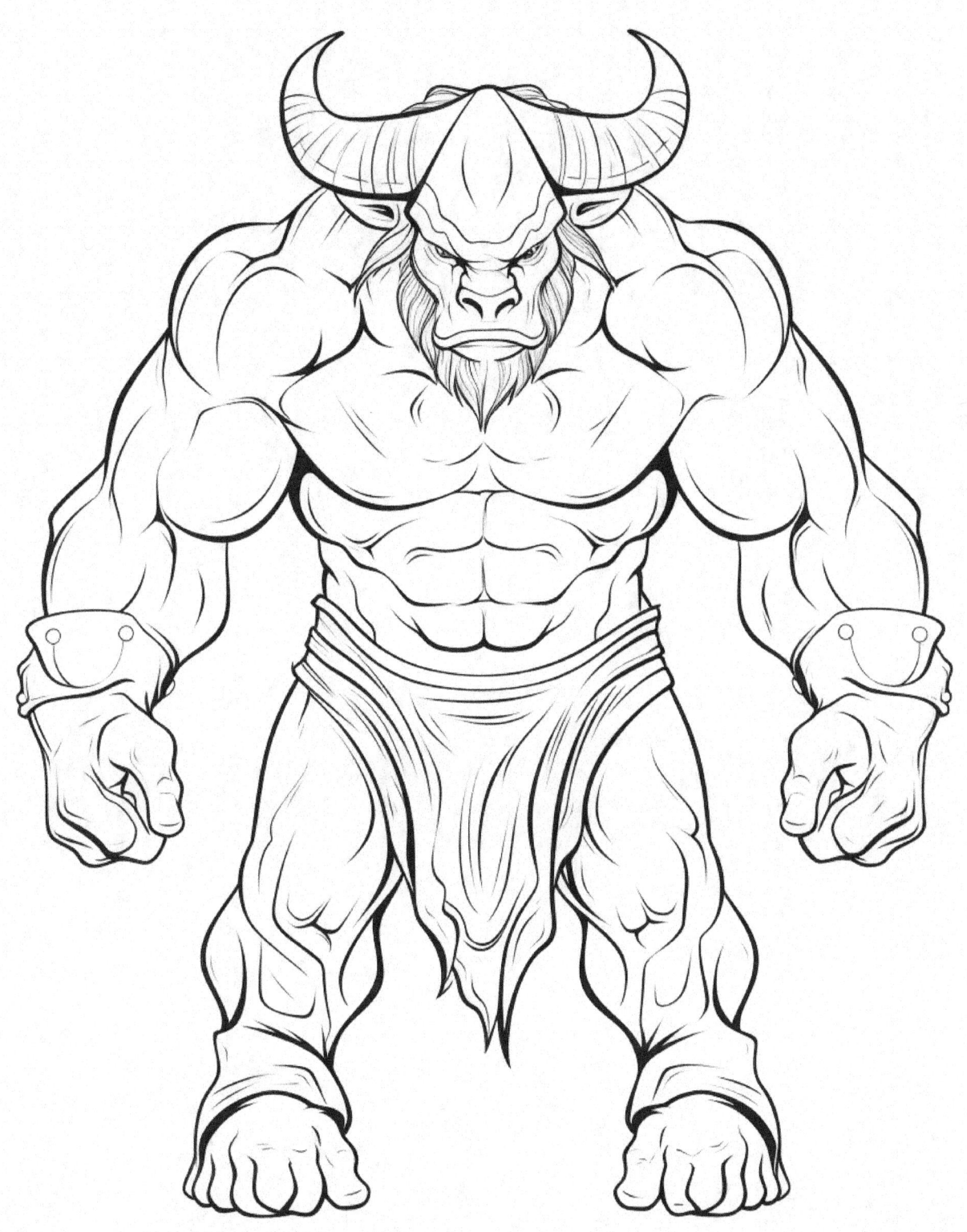

CHIMERA

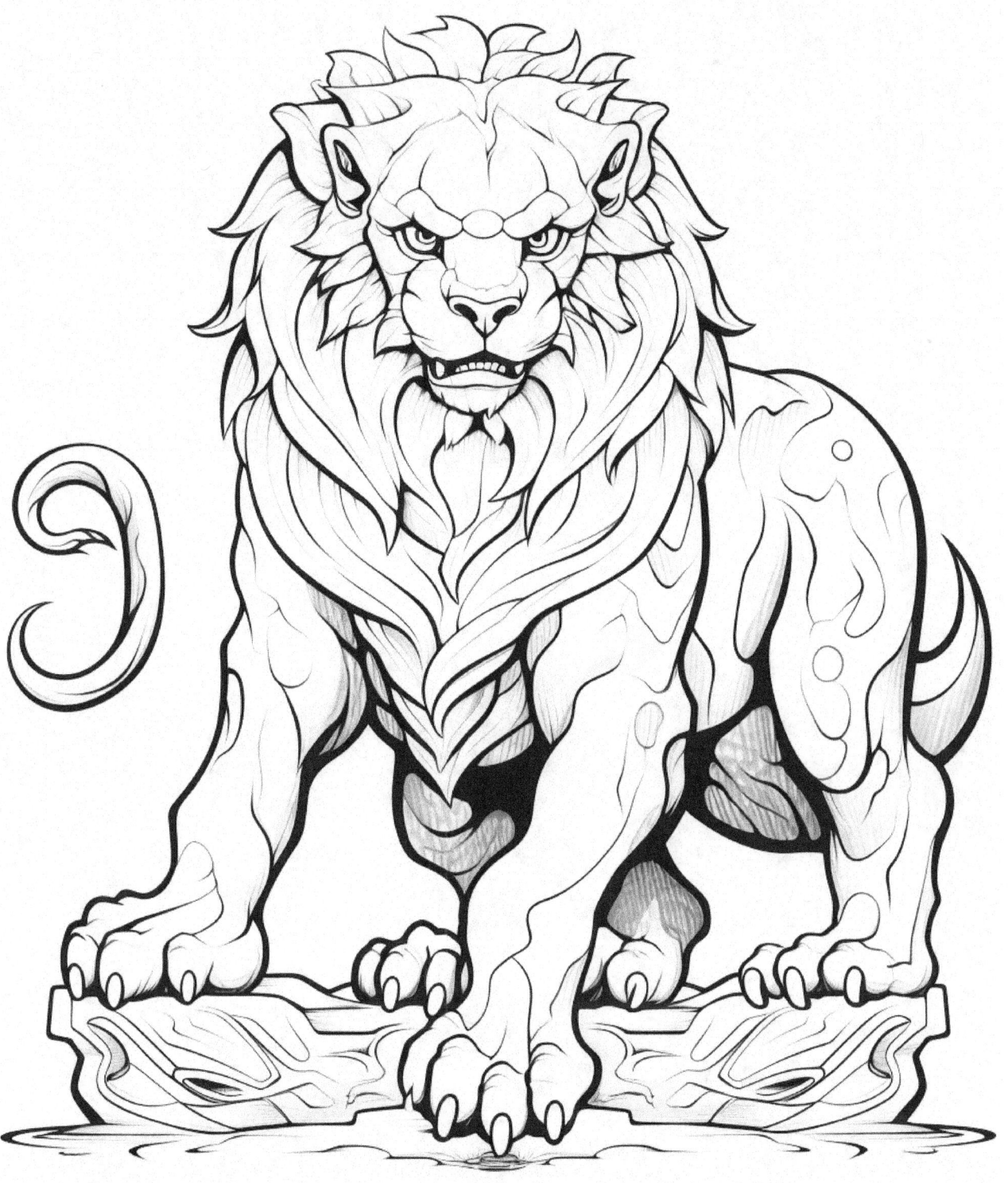

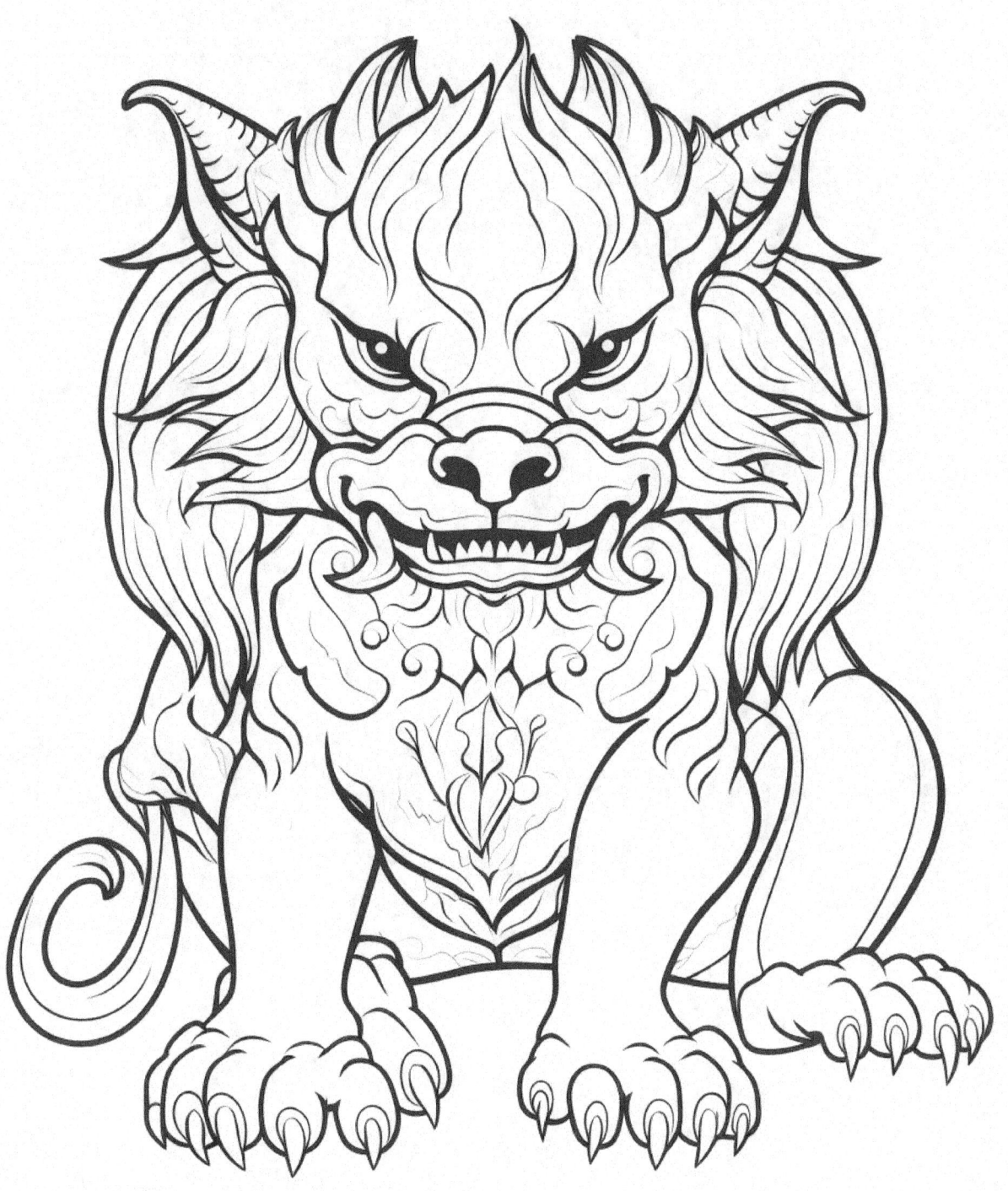

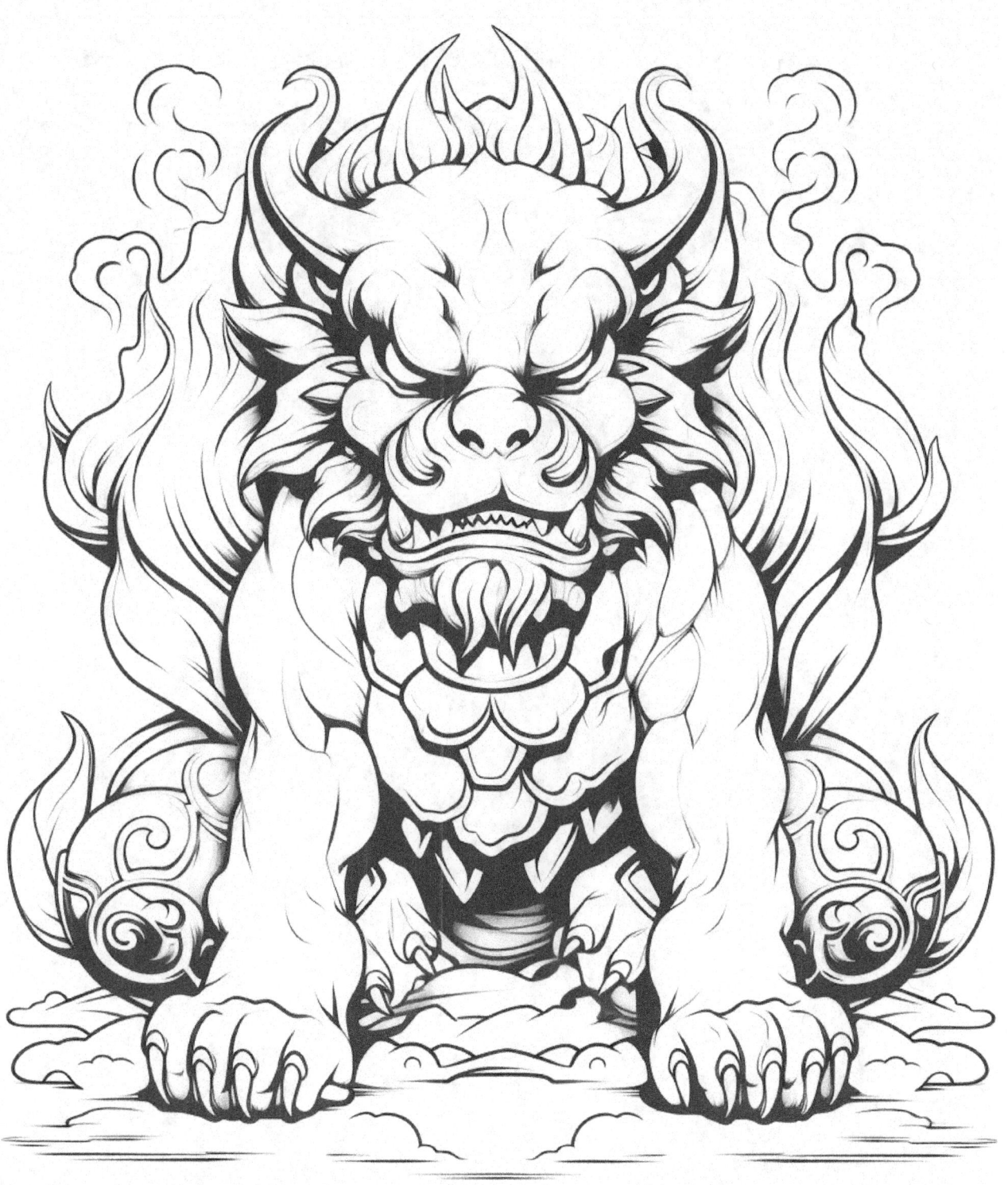

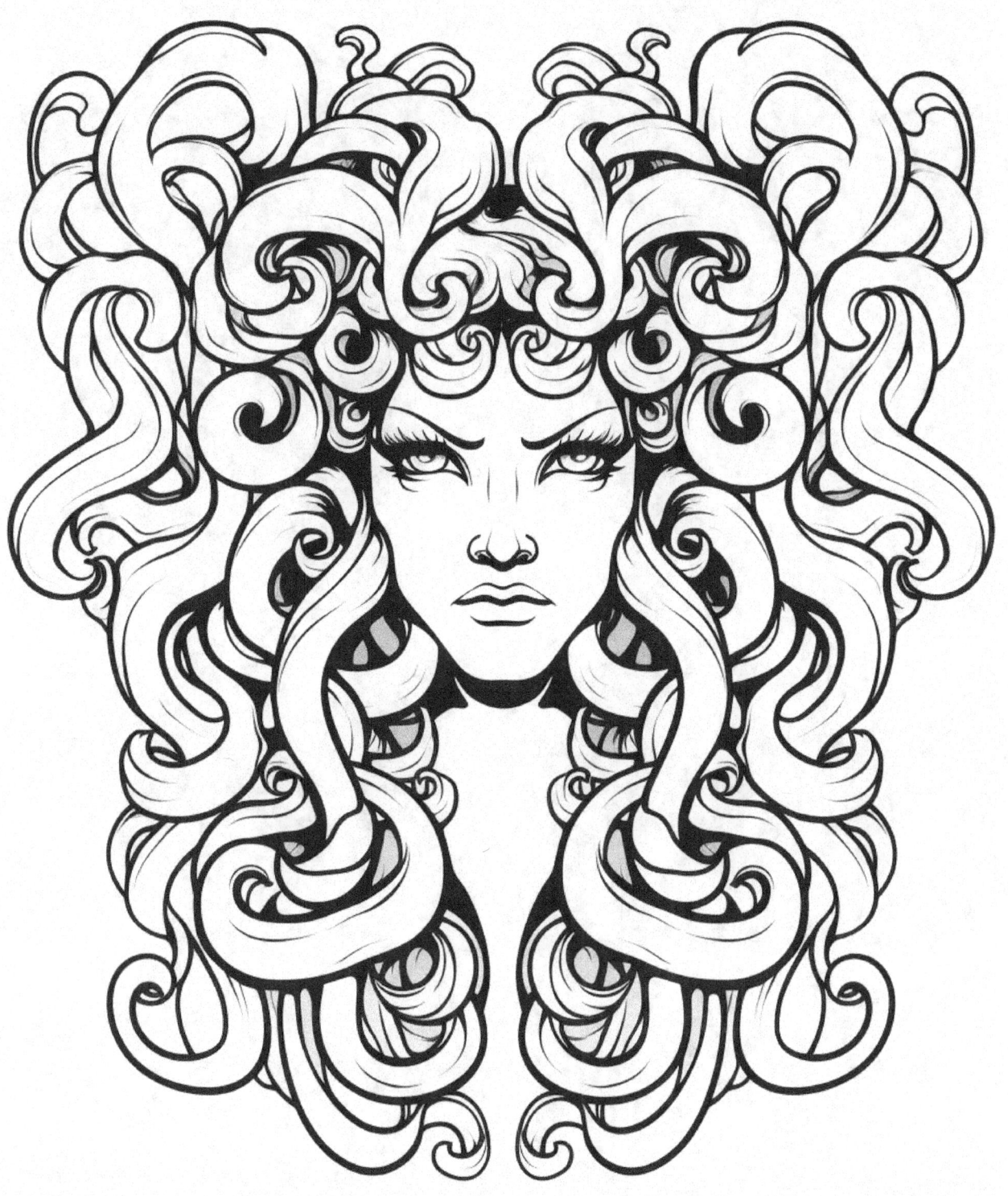

GORGON

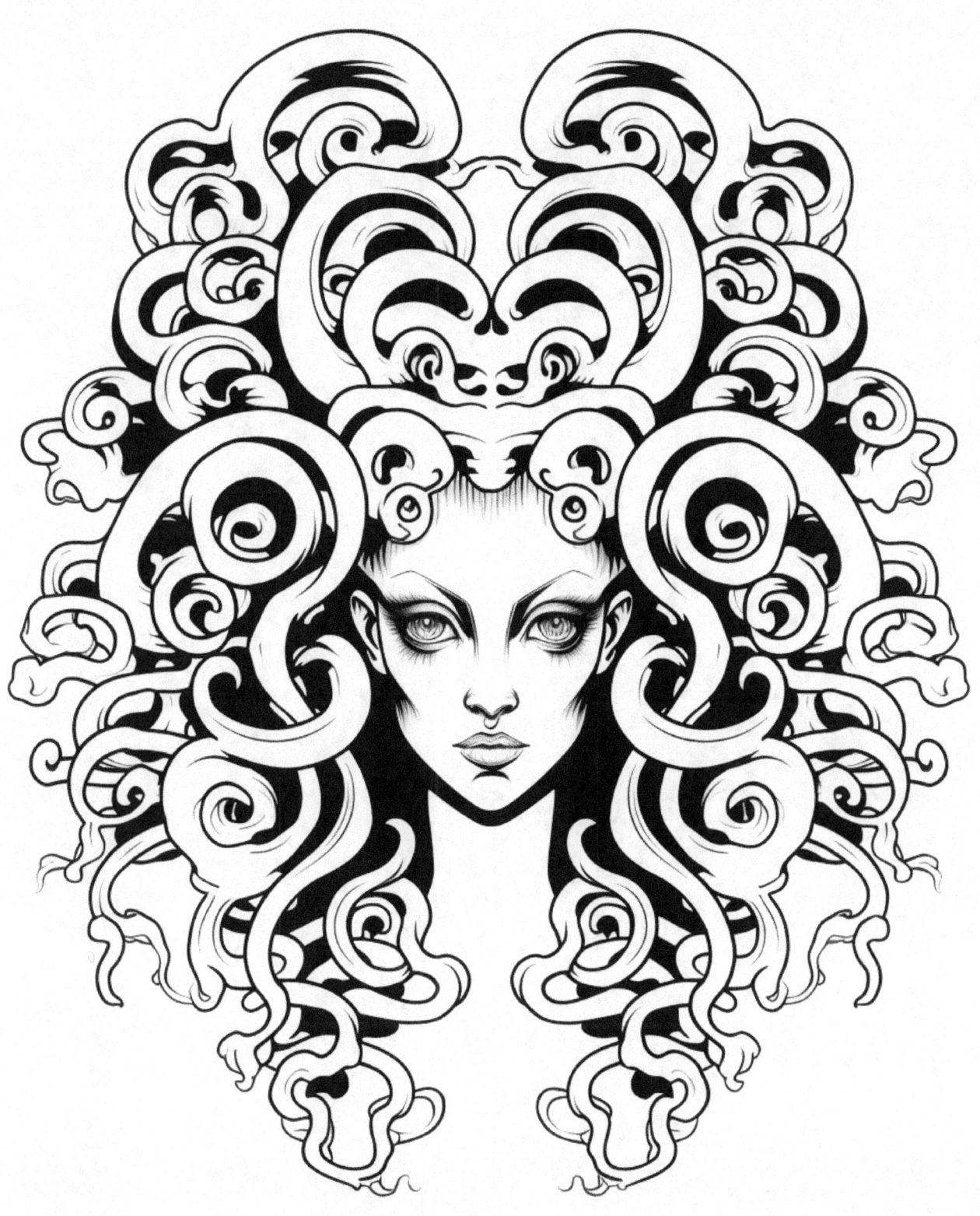

FAIRY DRAGON

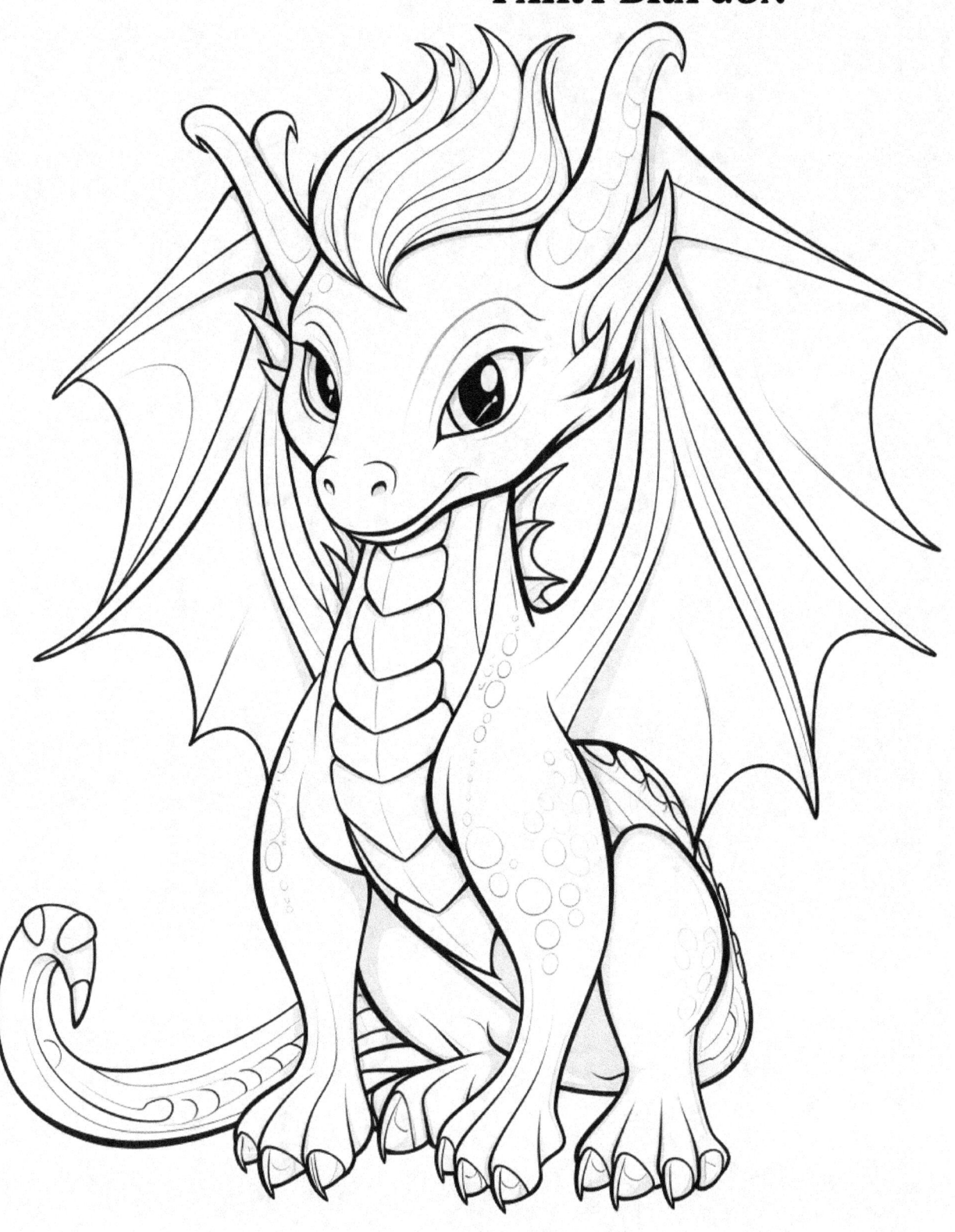

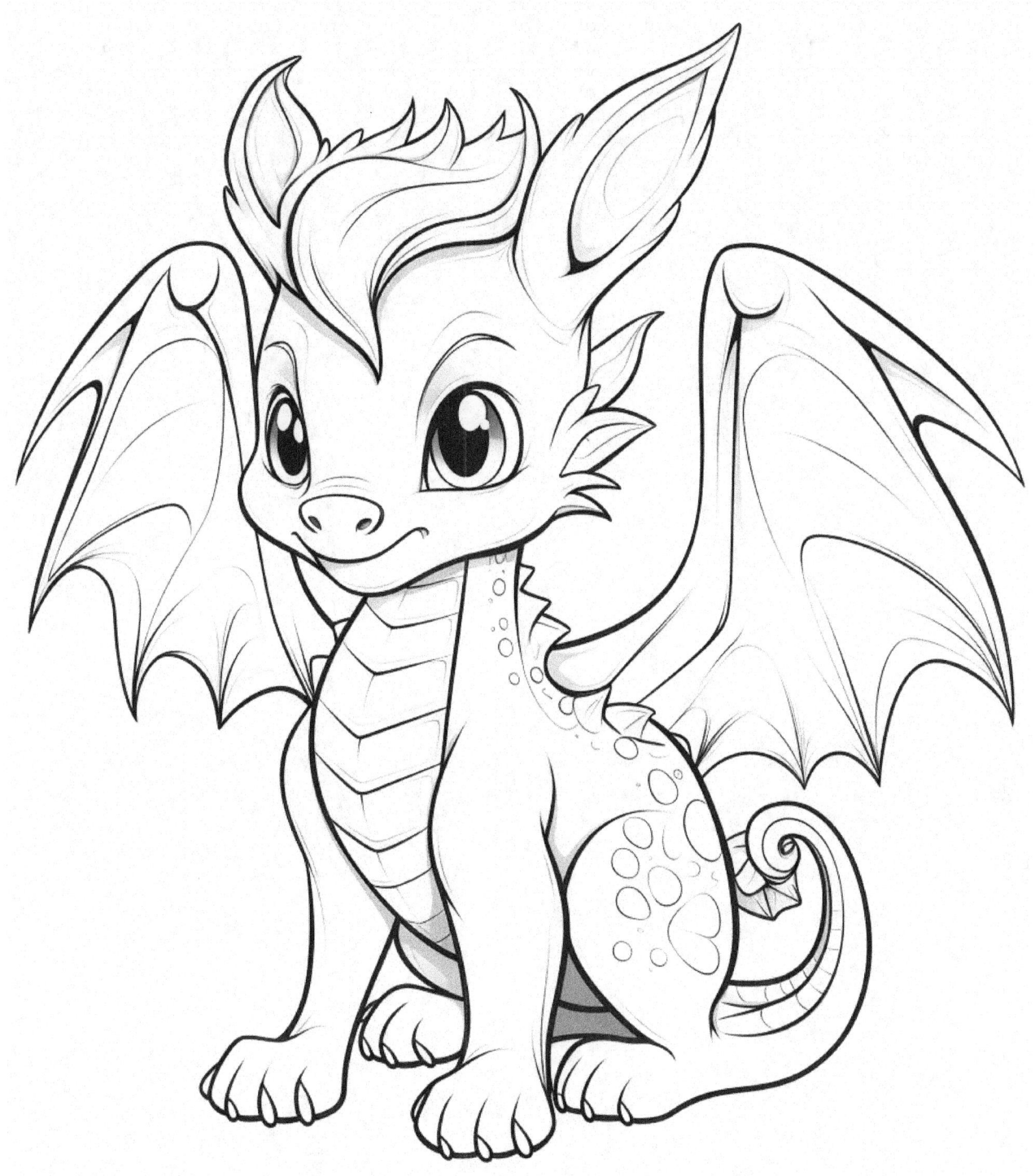

NYMPH

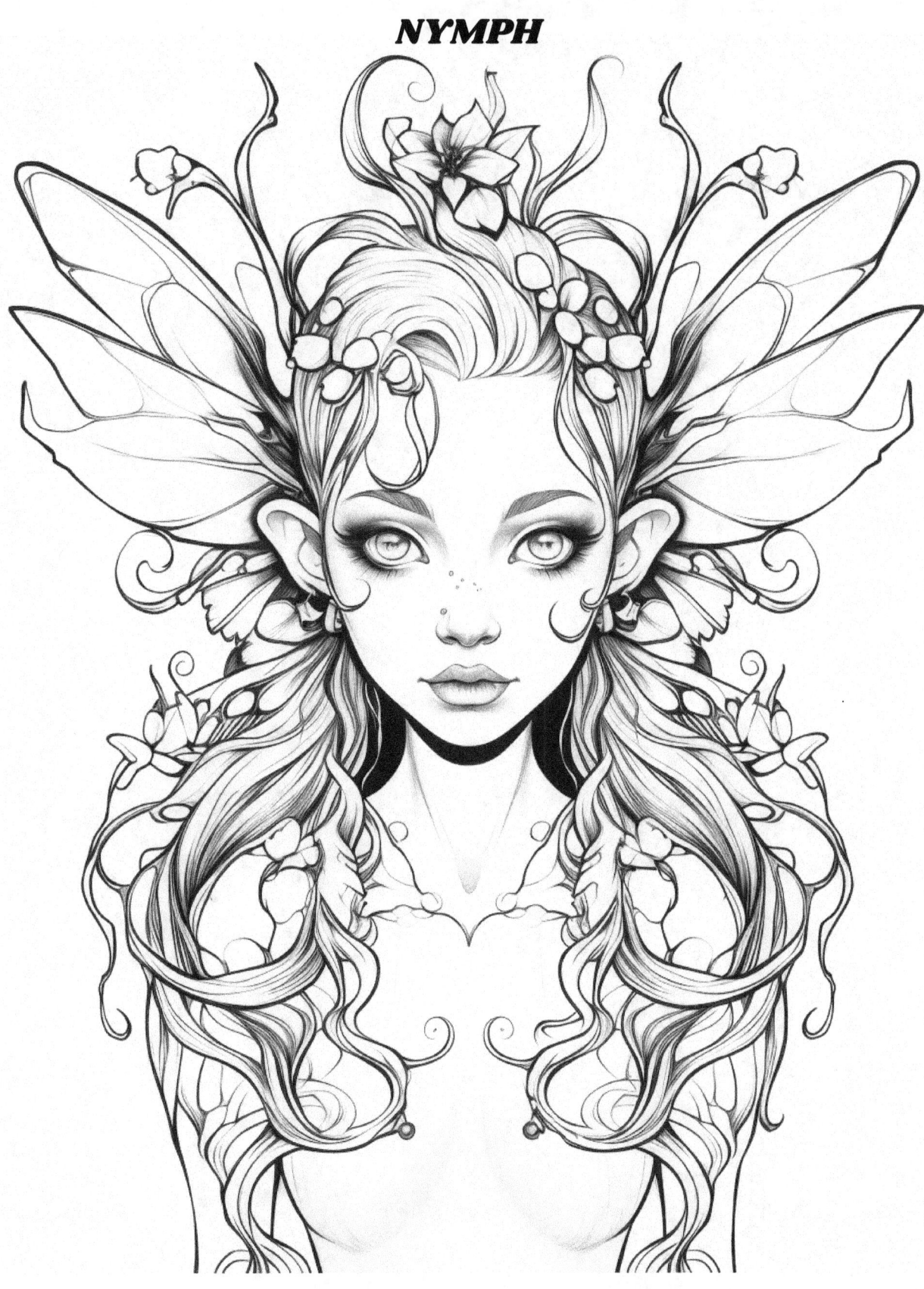

TROLL

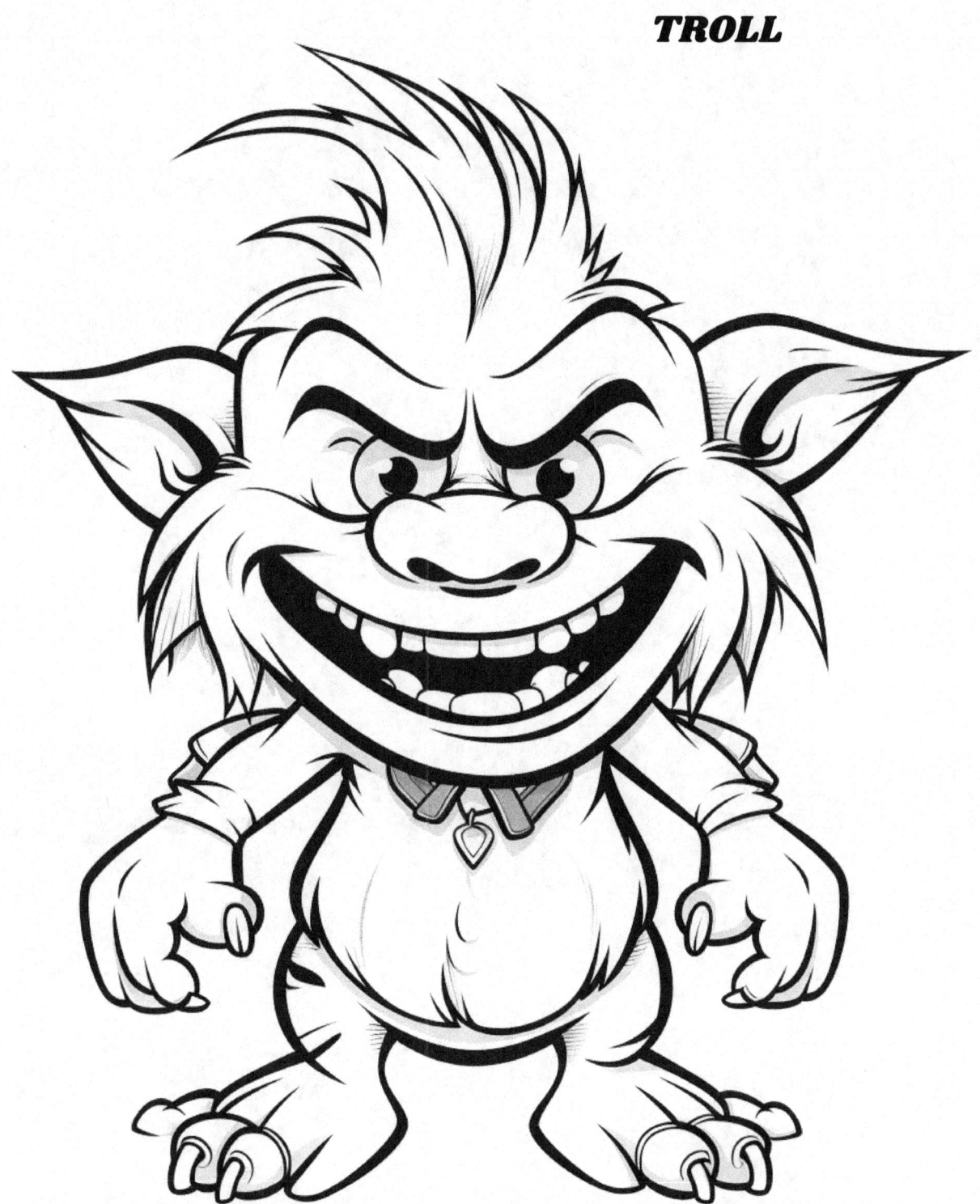

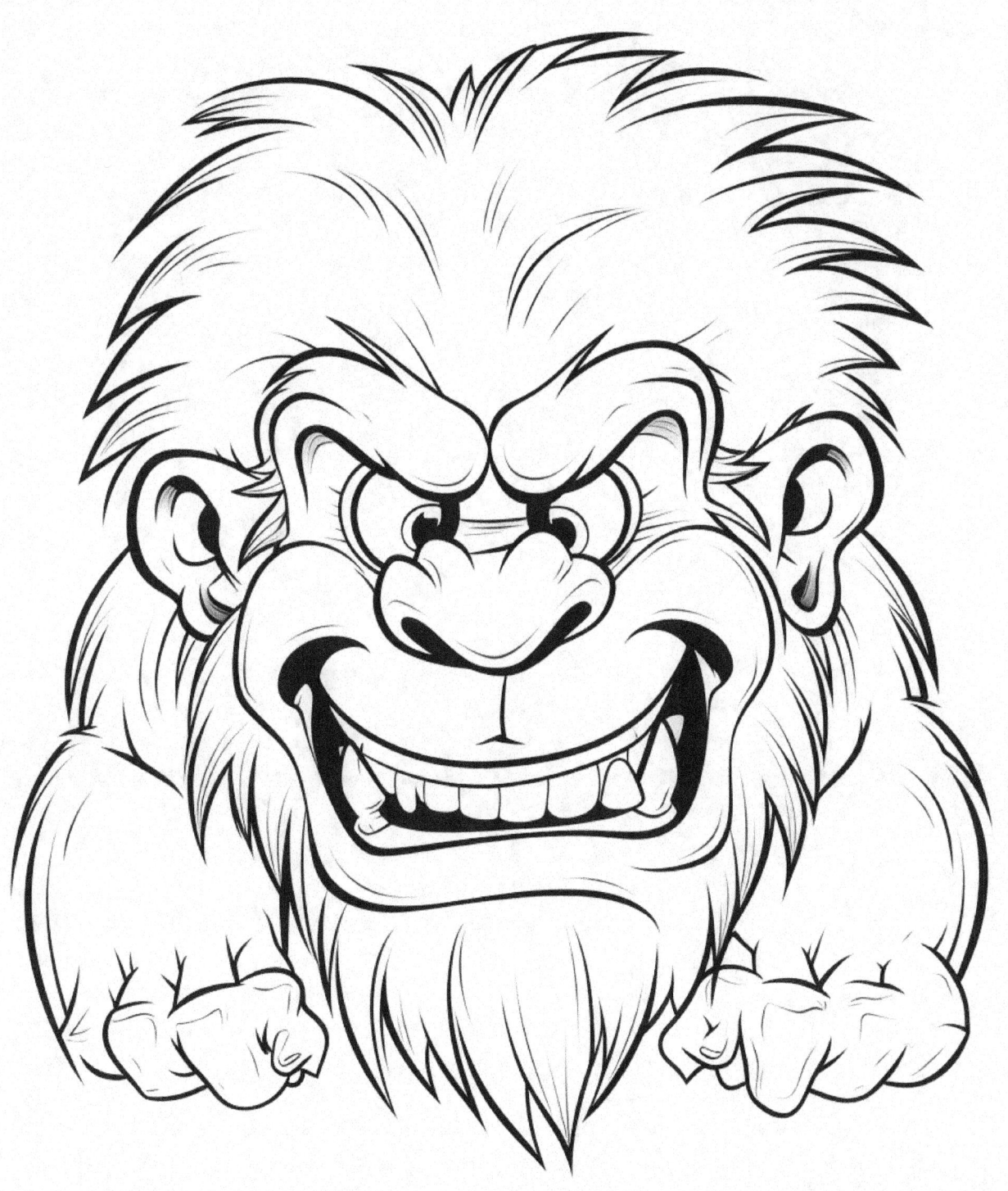

HARPY

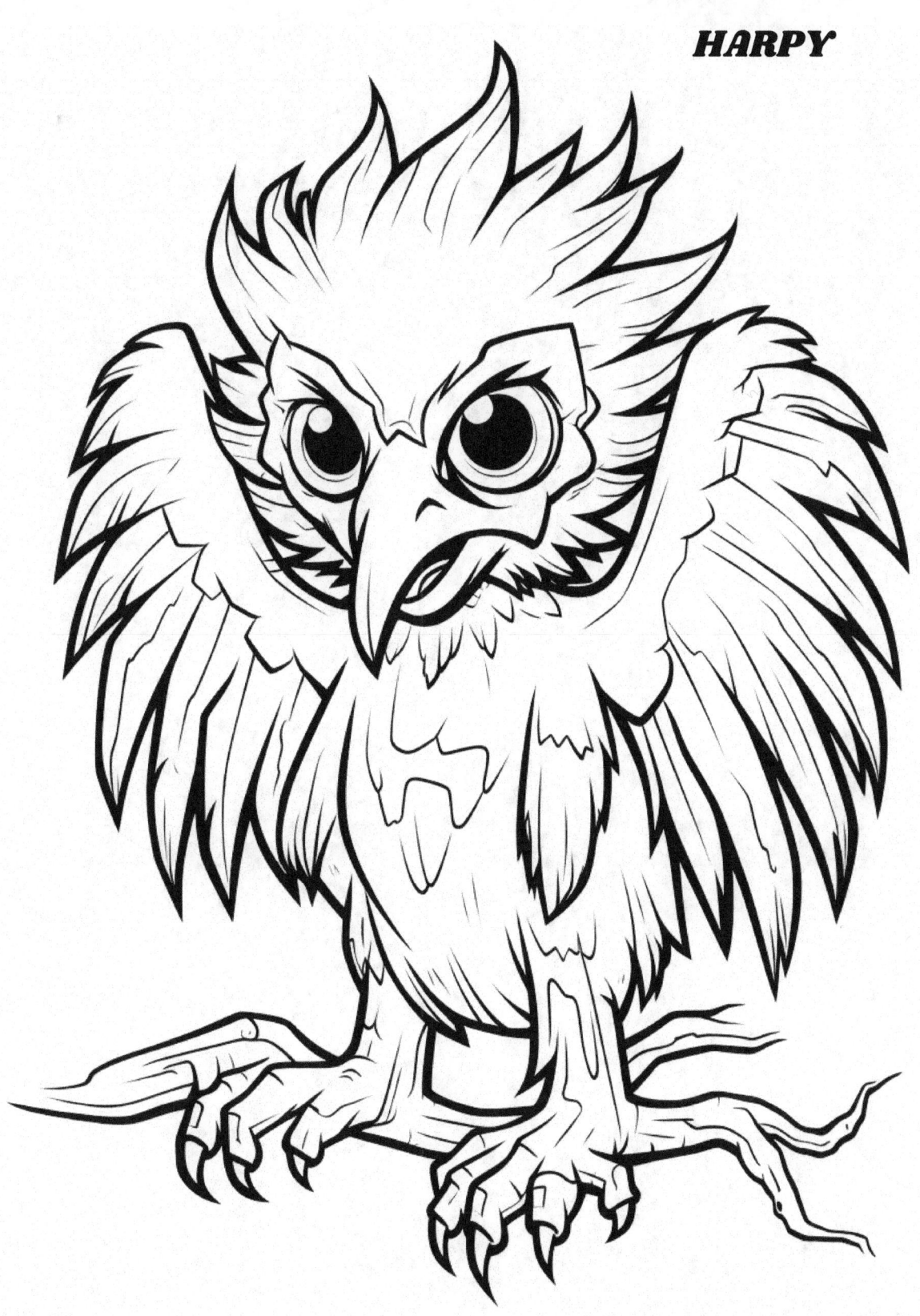

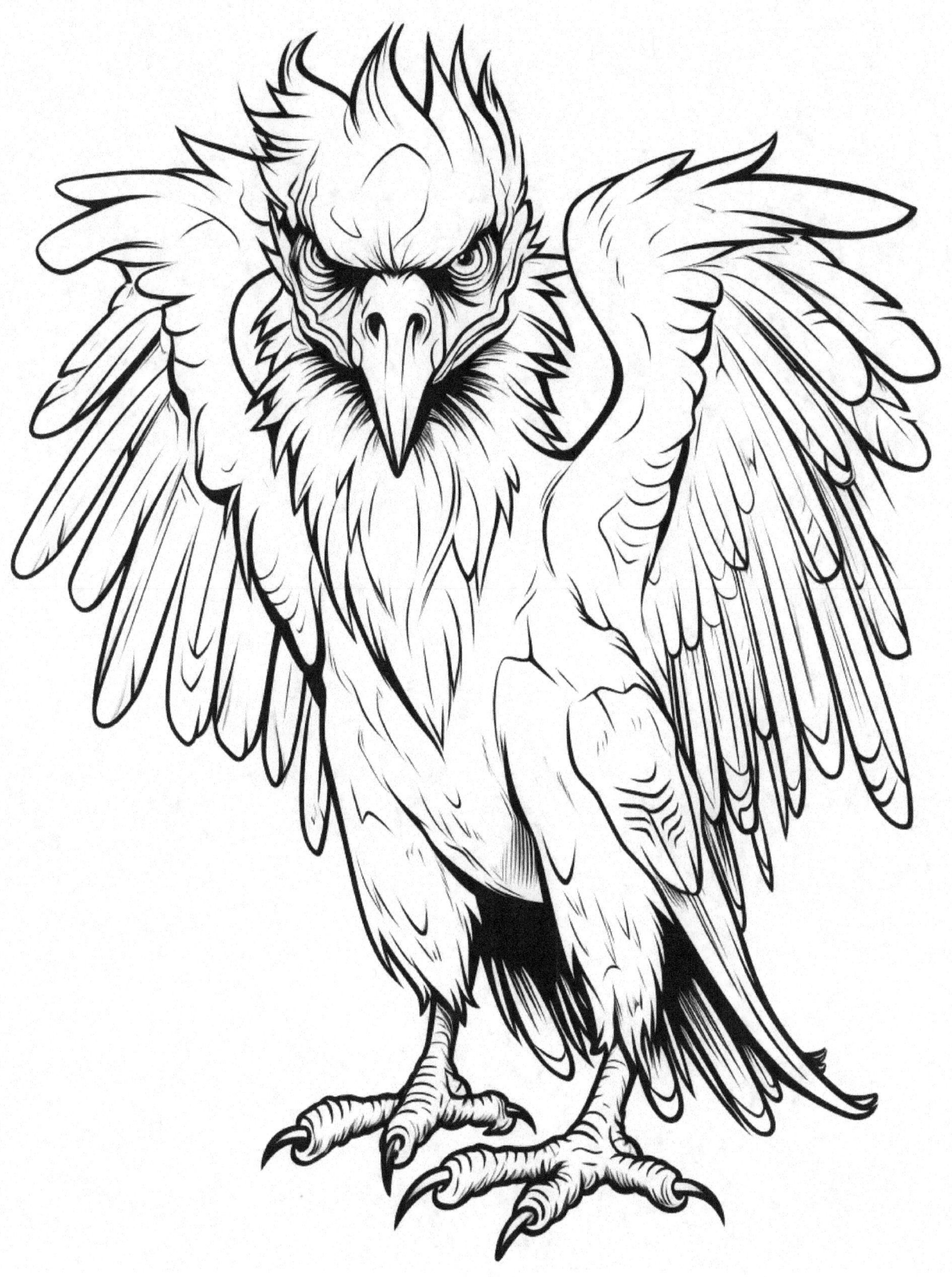

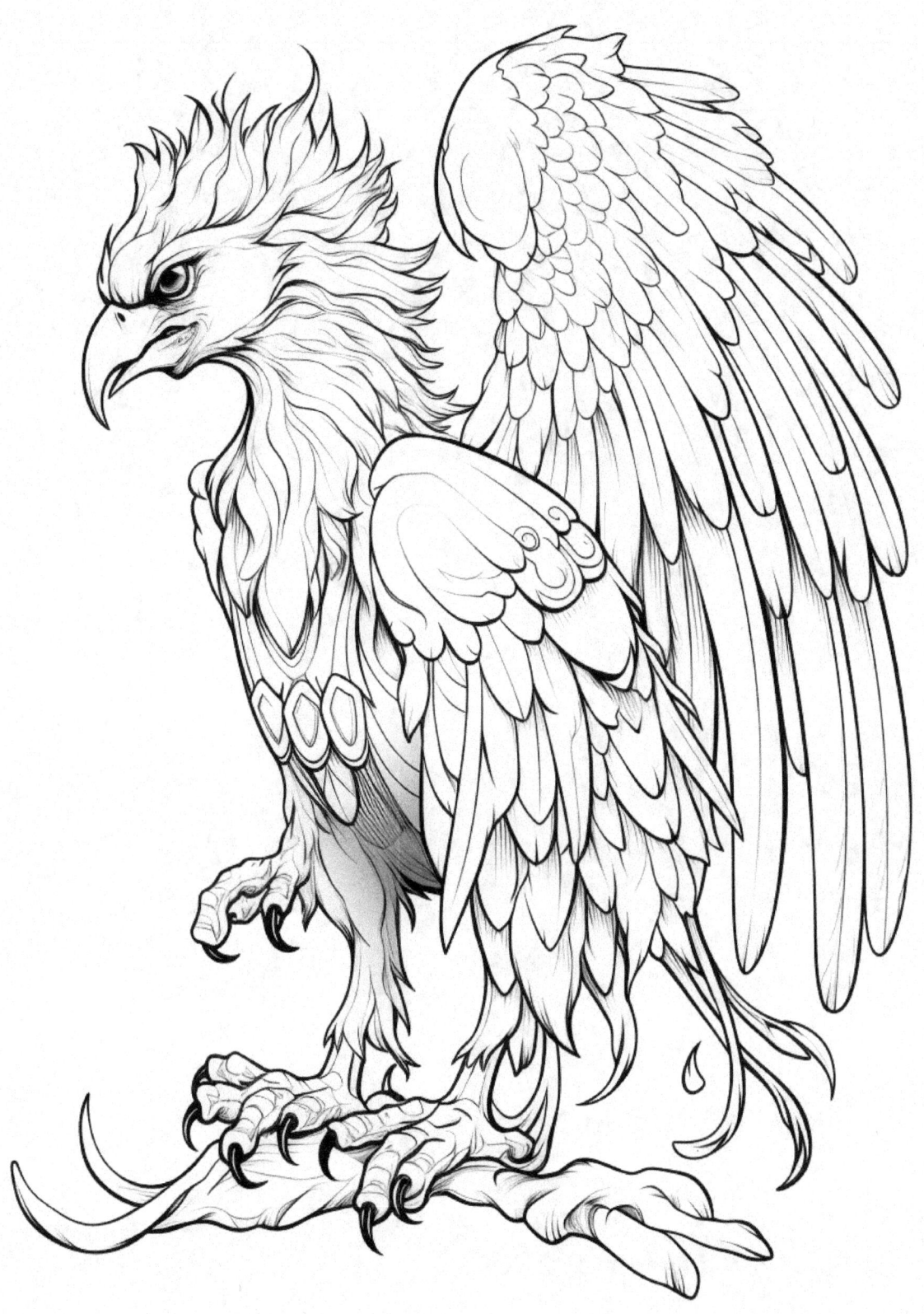

TROLL

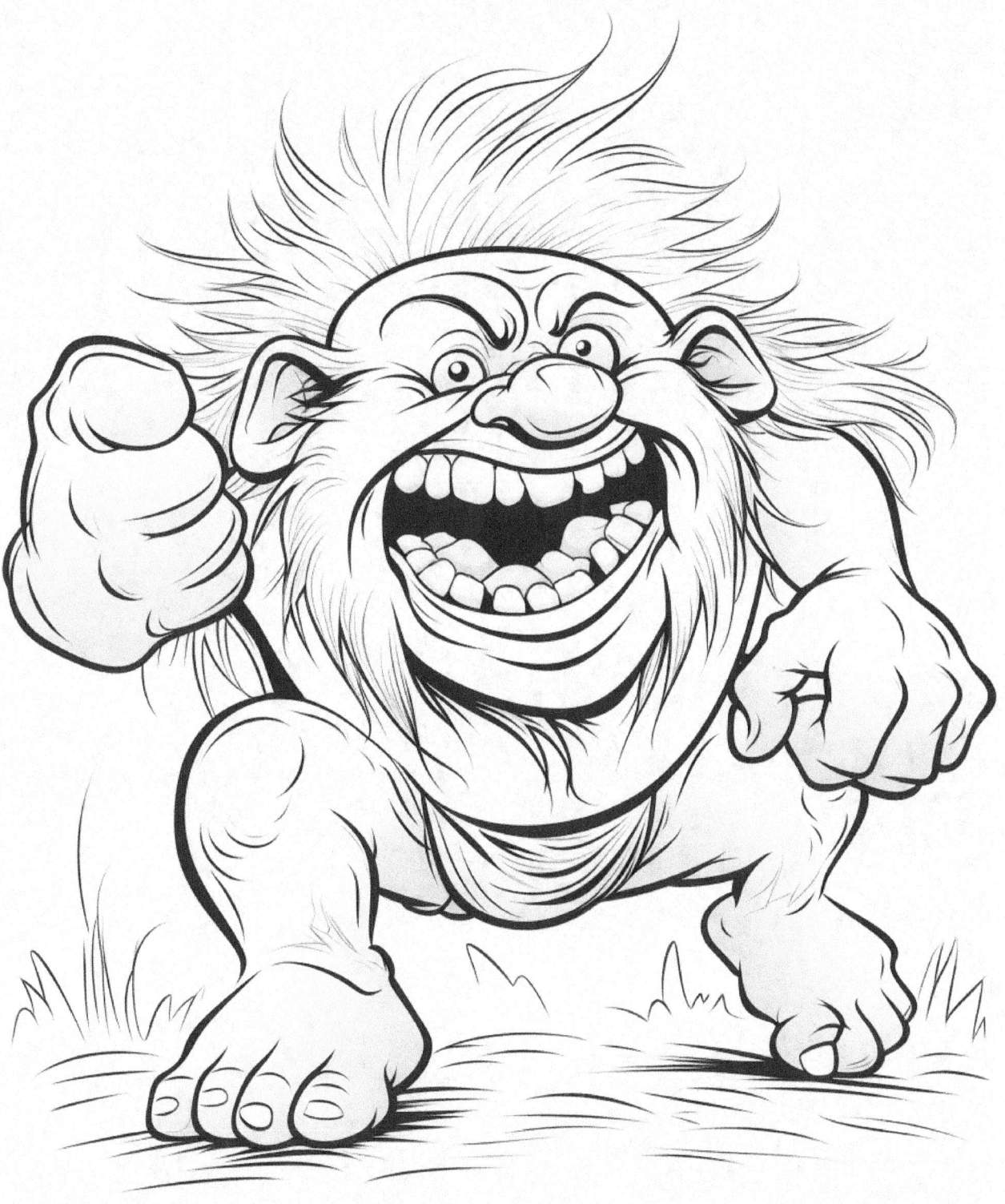

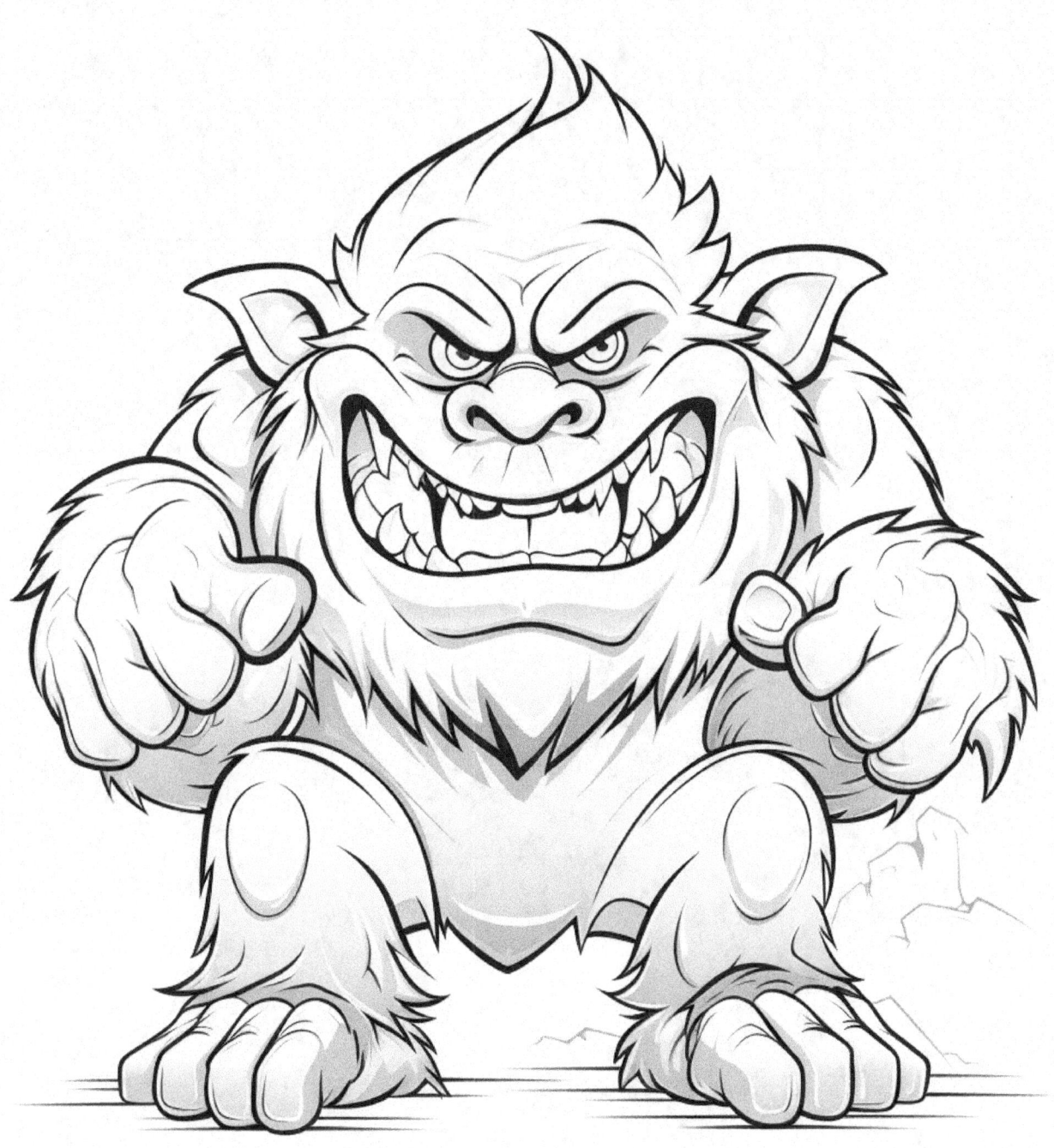

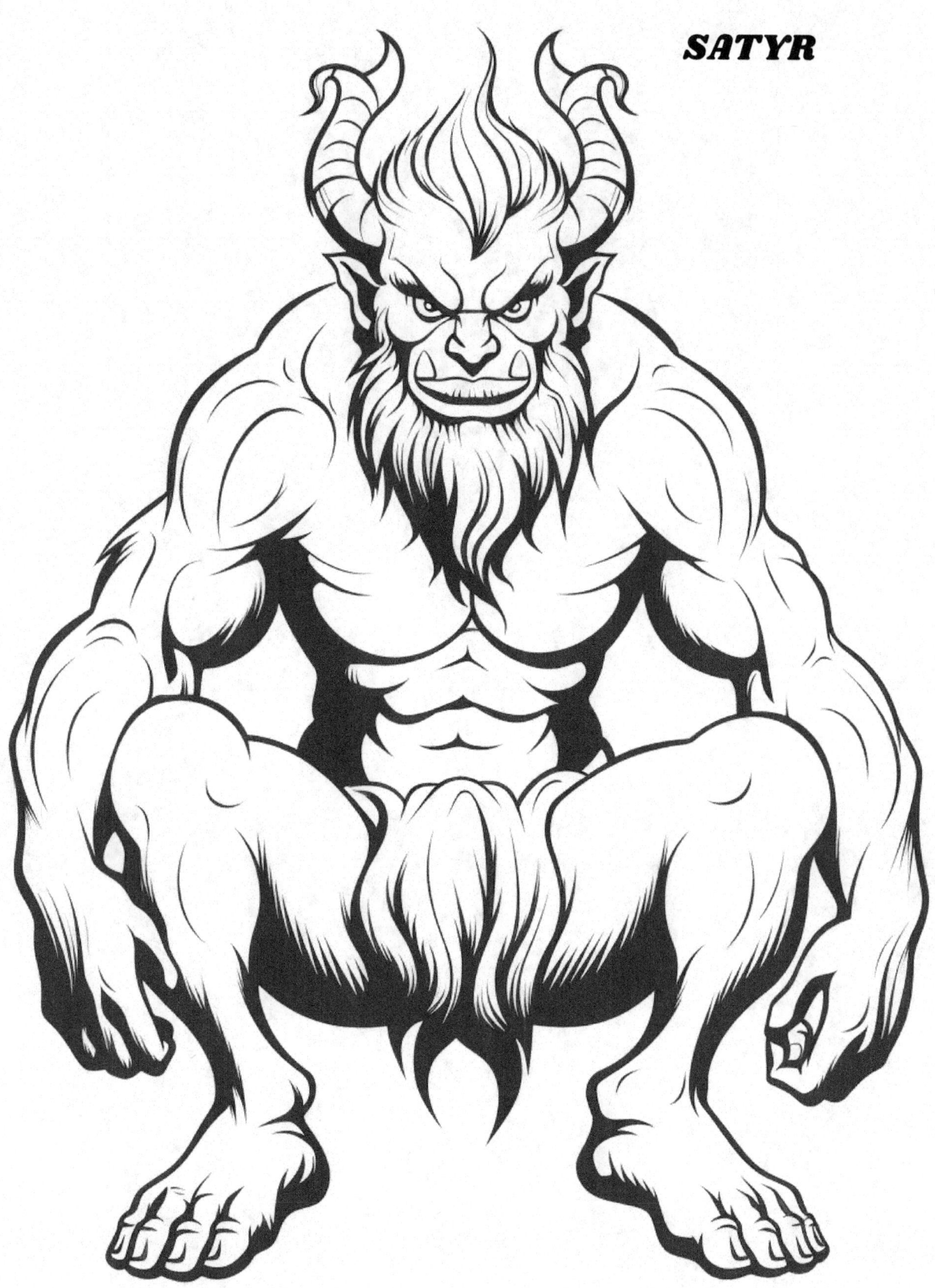

SATYR

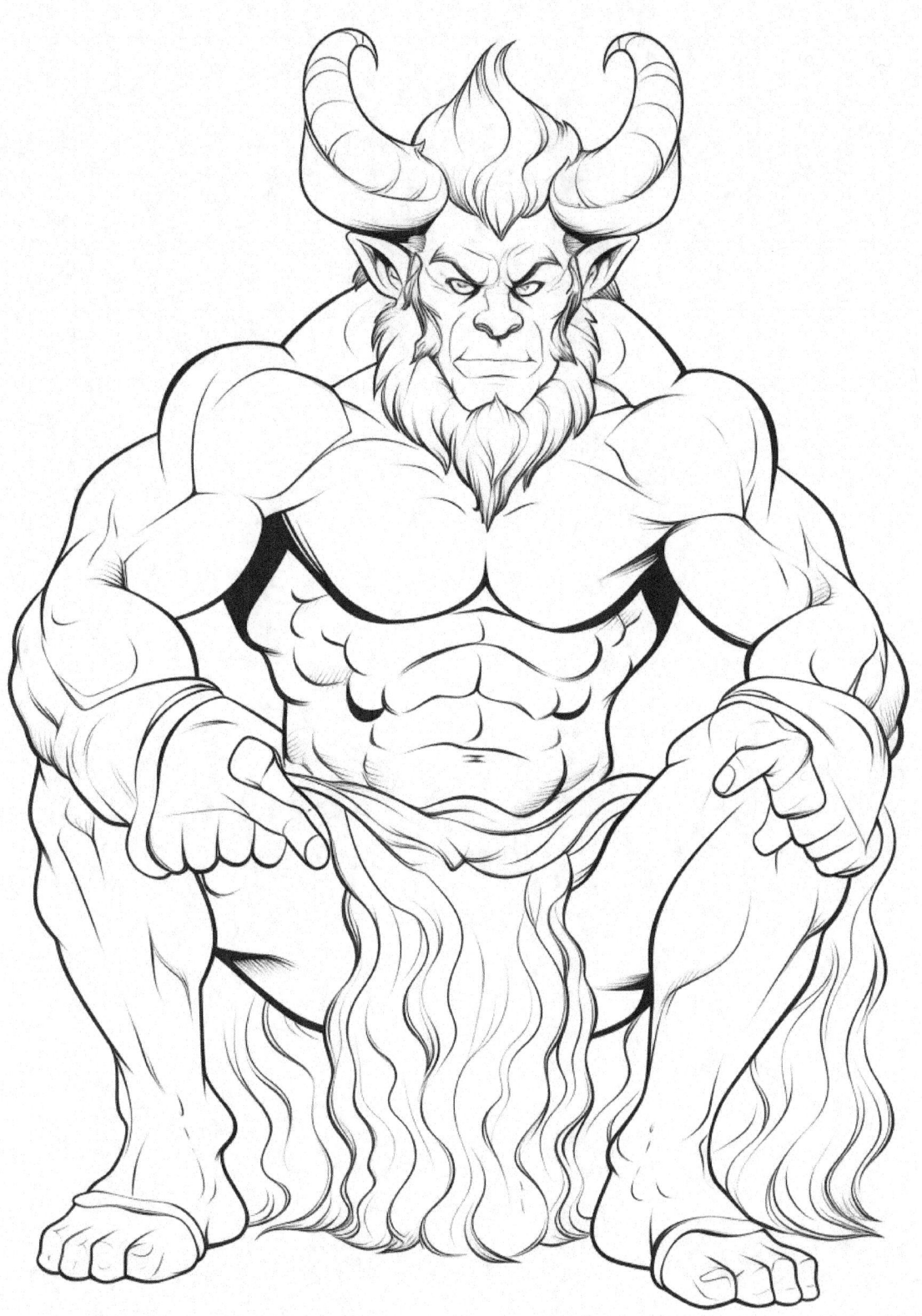

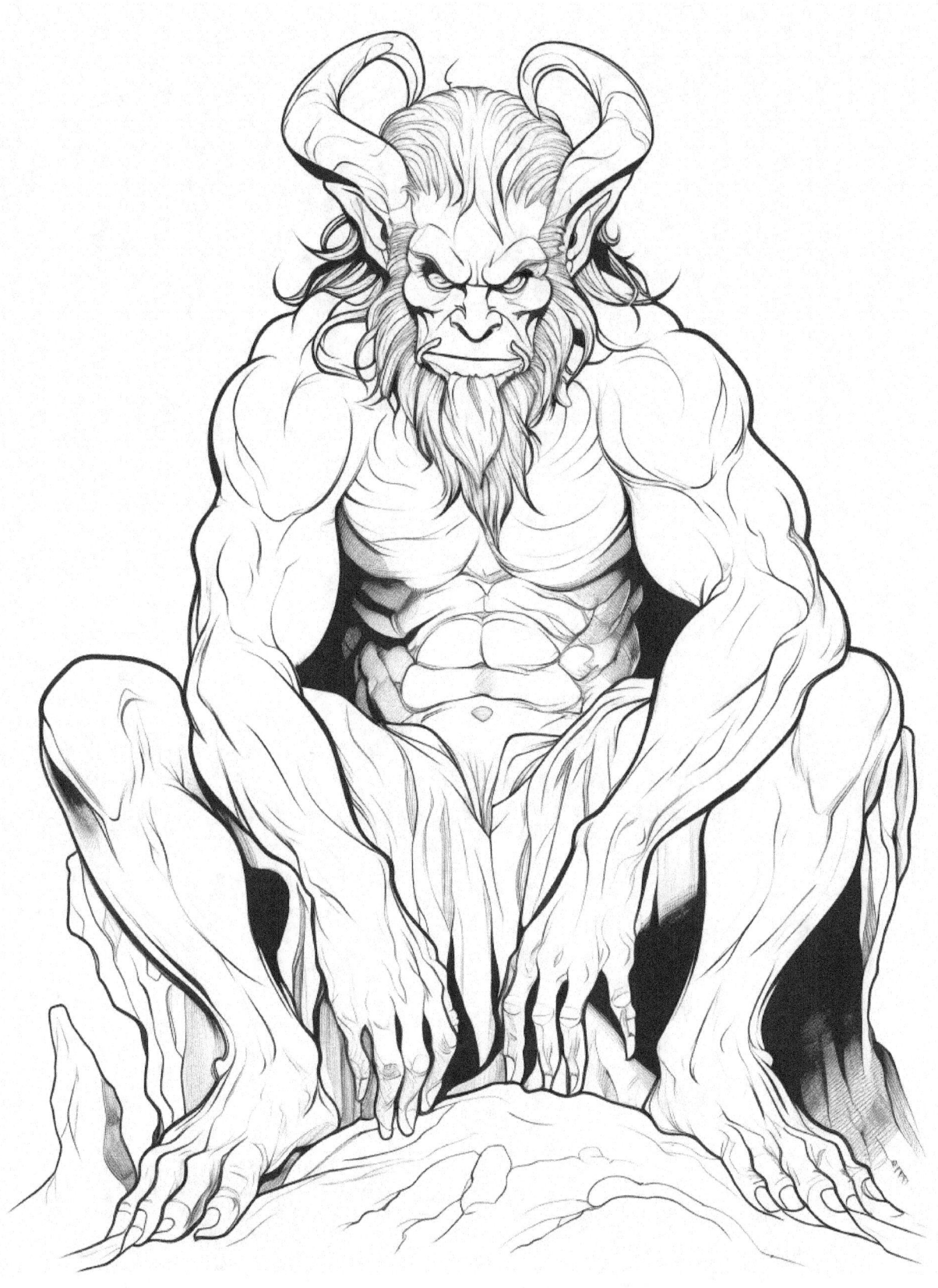

SYLPH

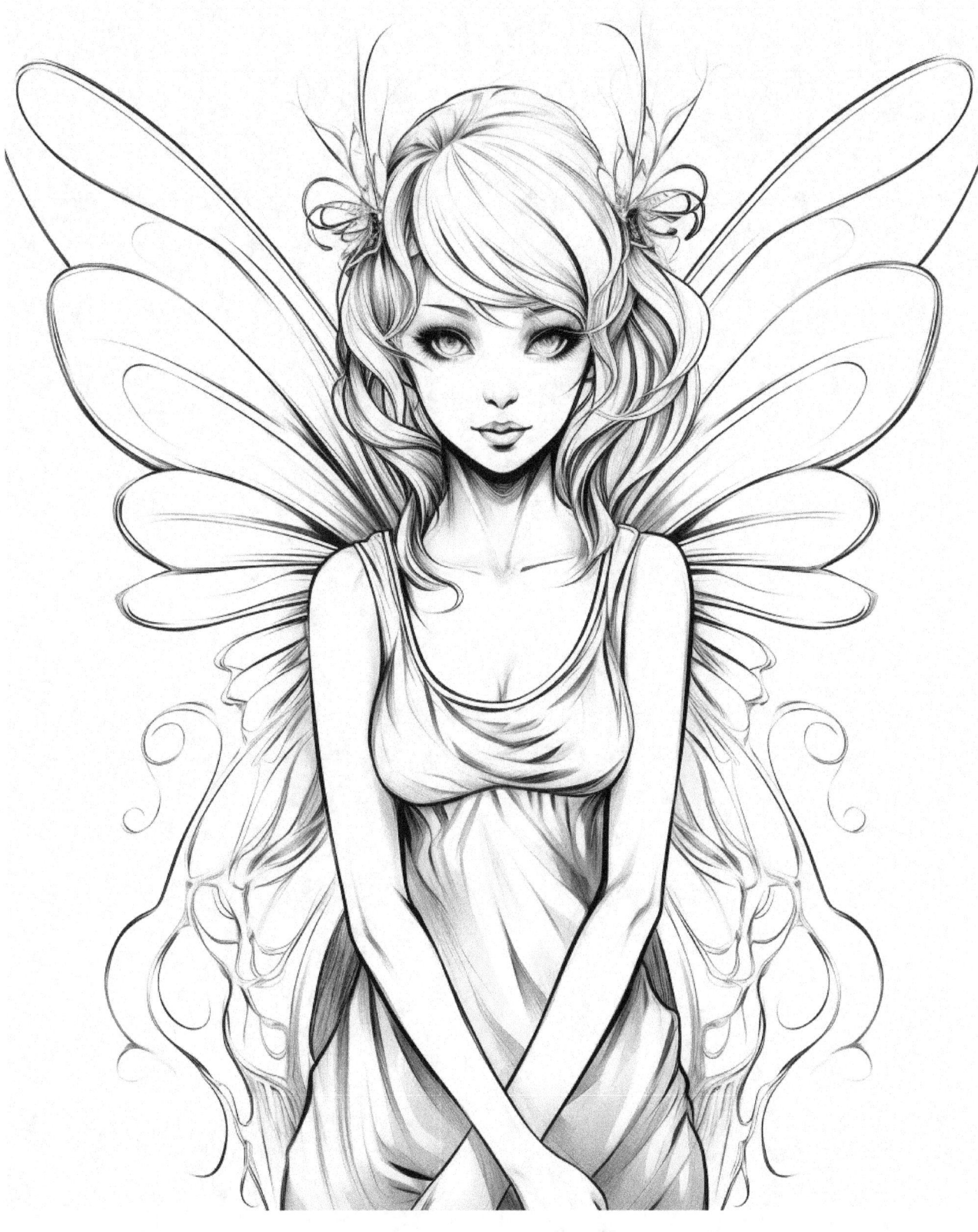

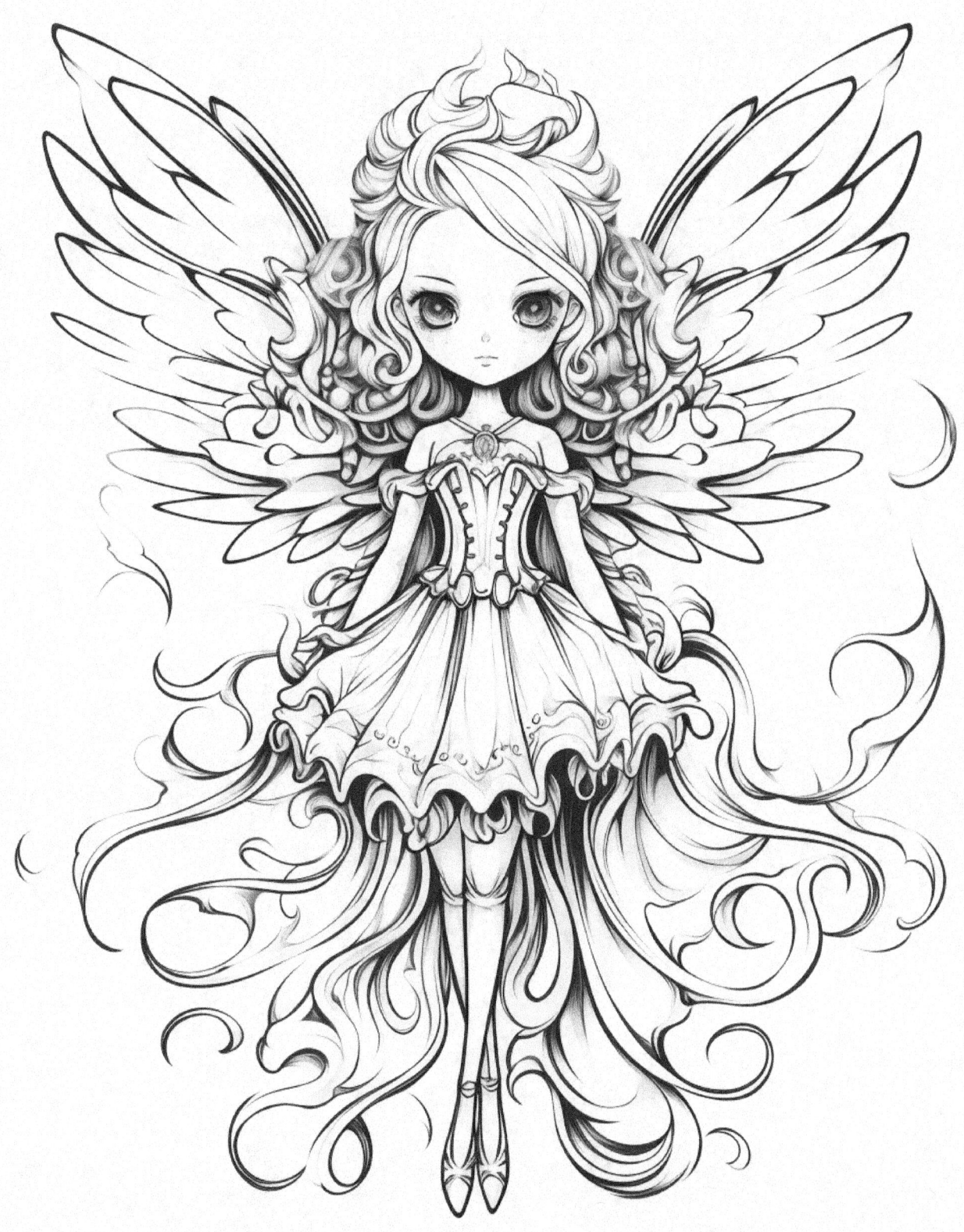

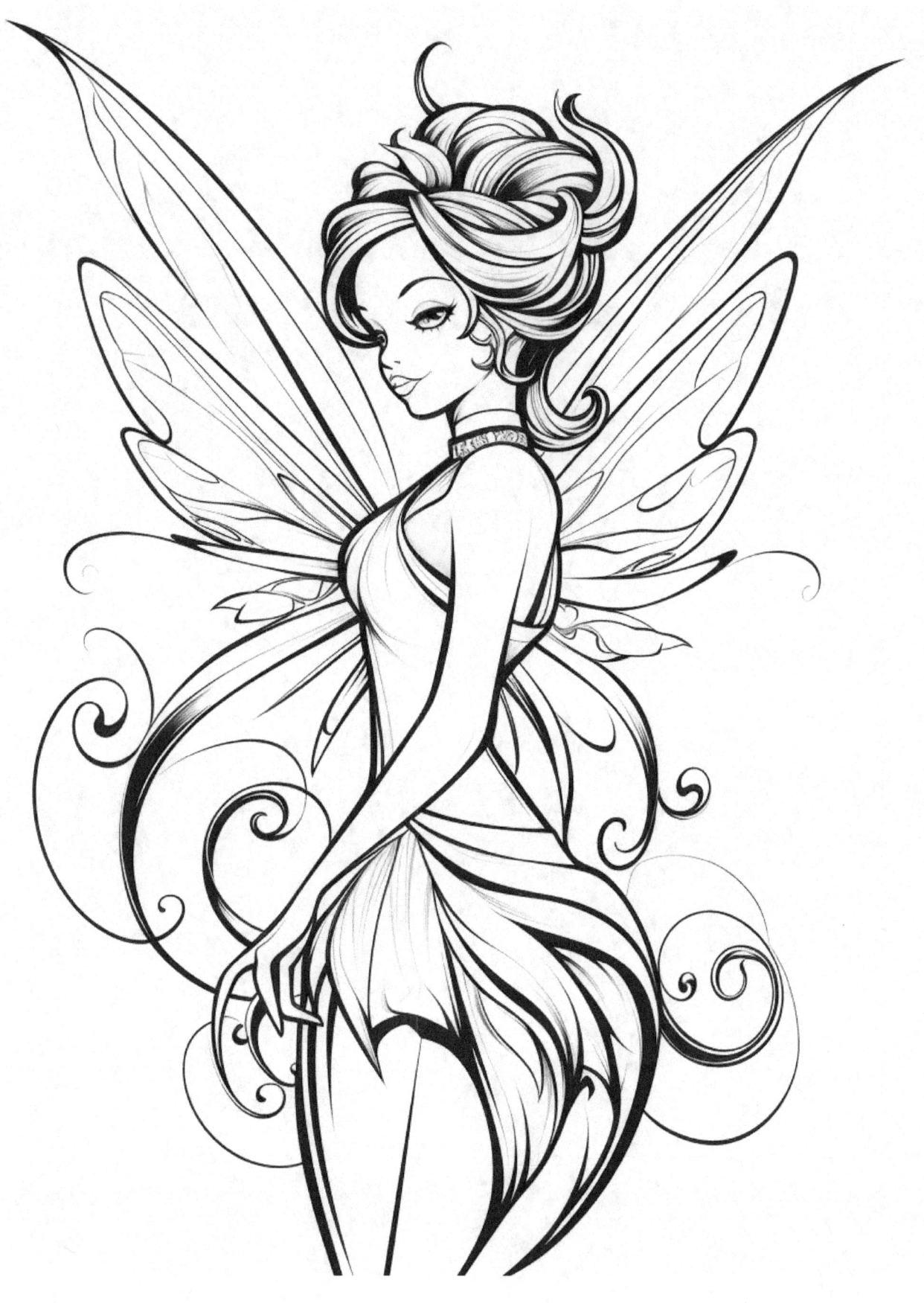

SPHINX

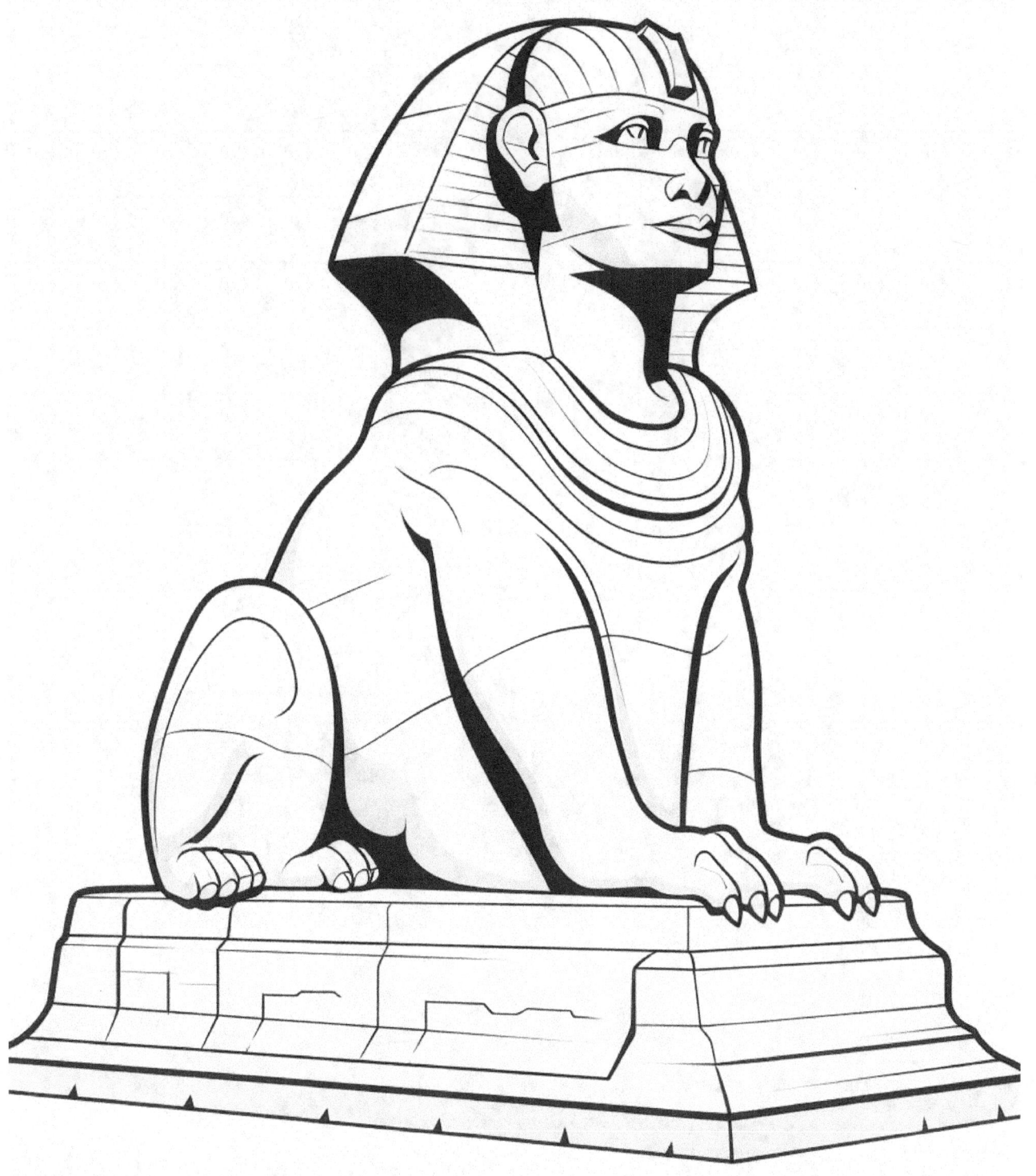

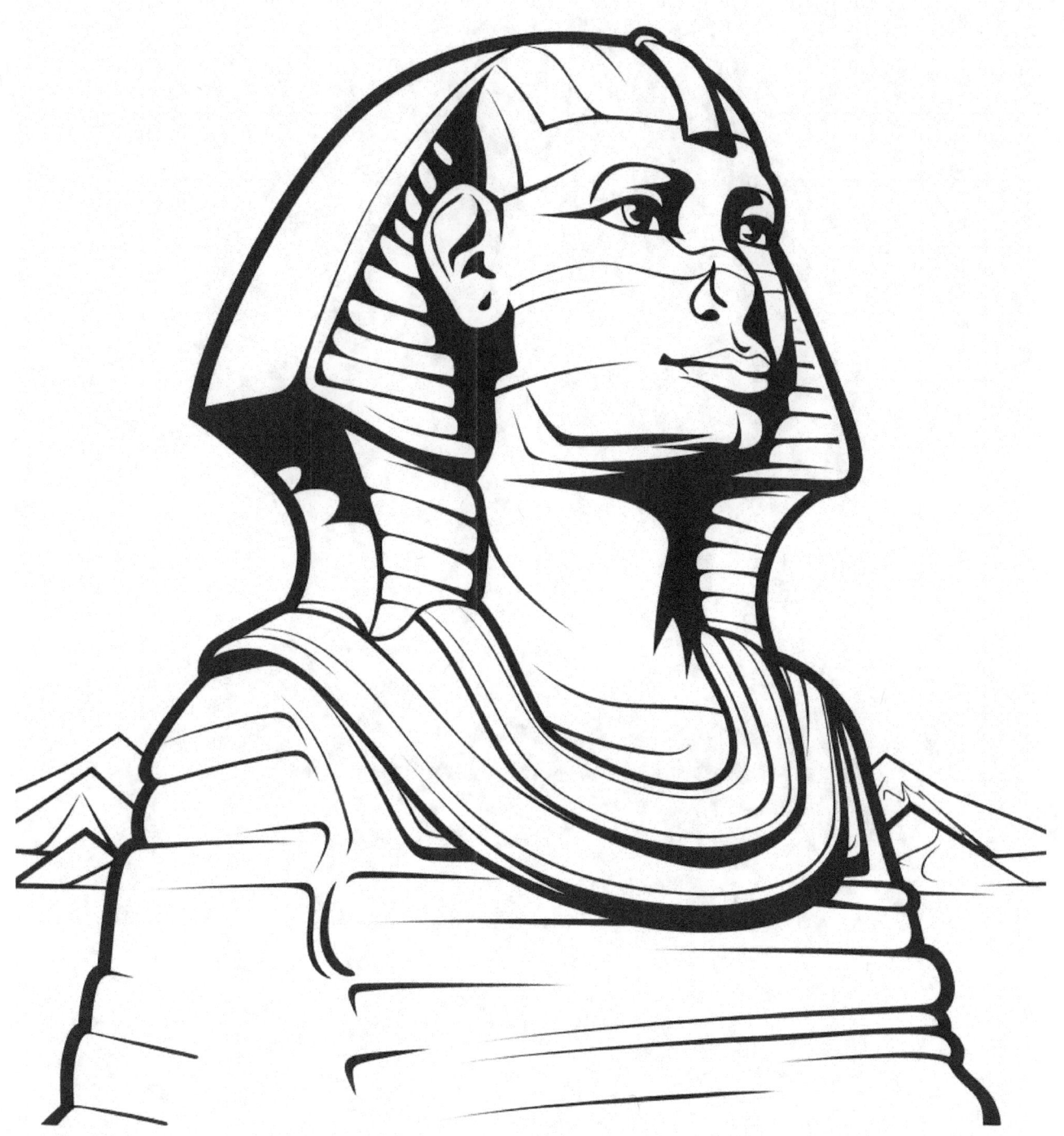

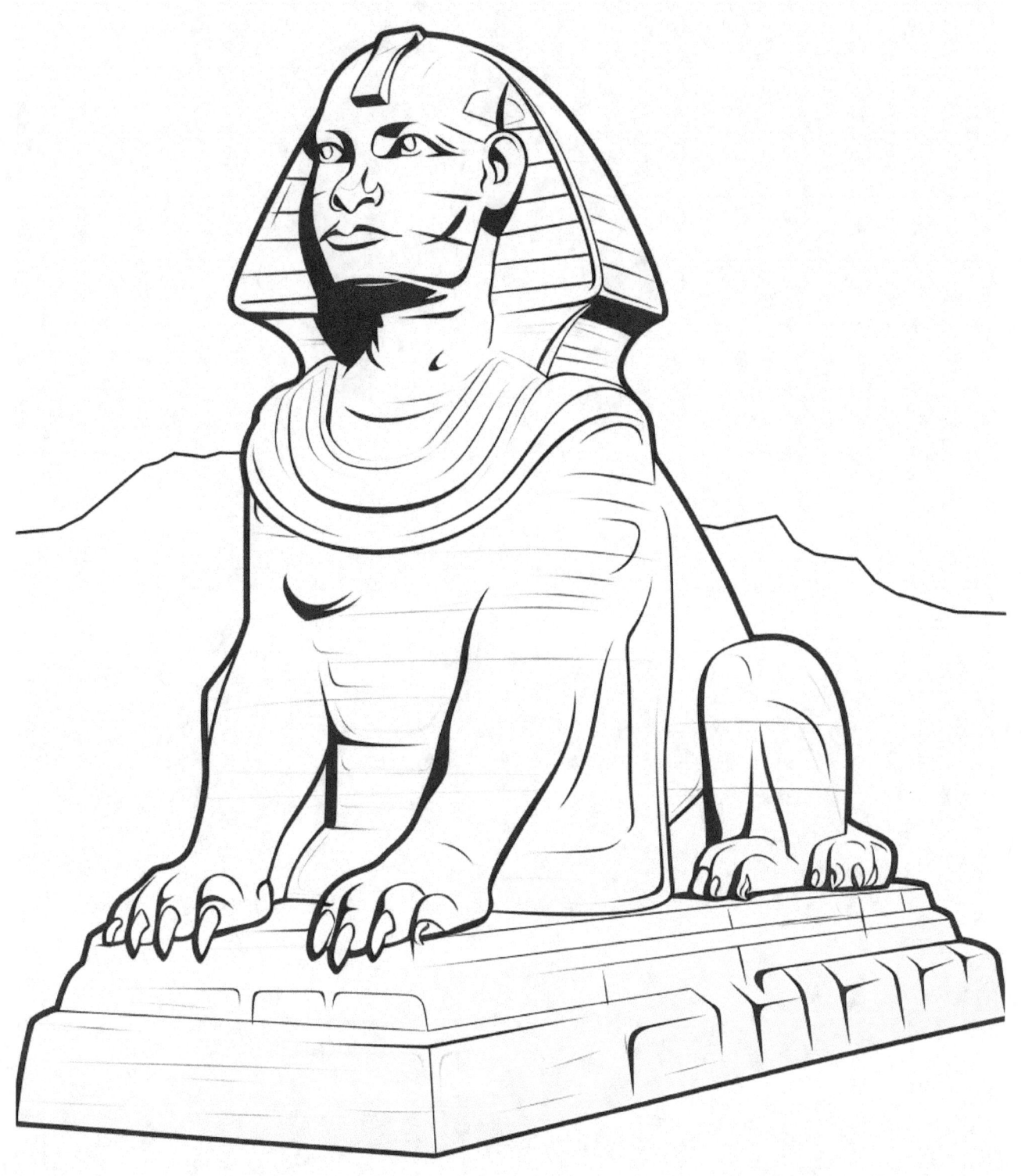

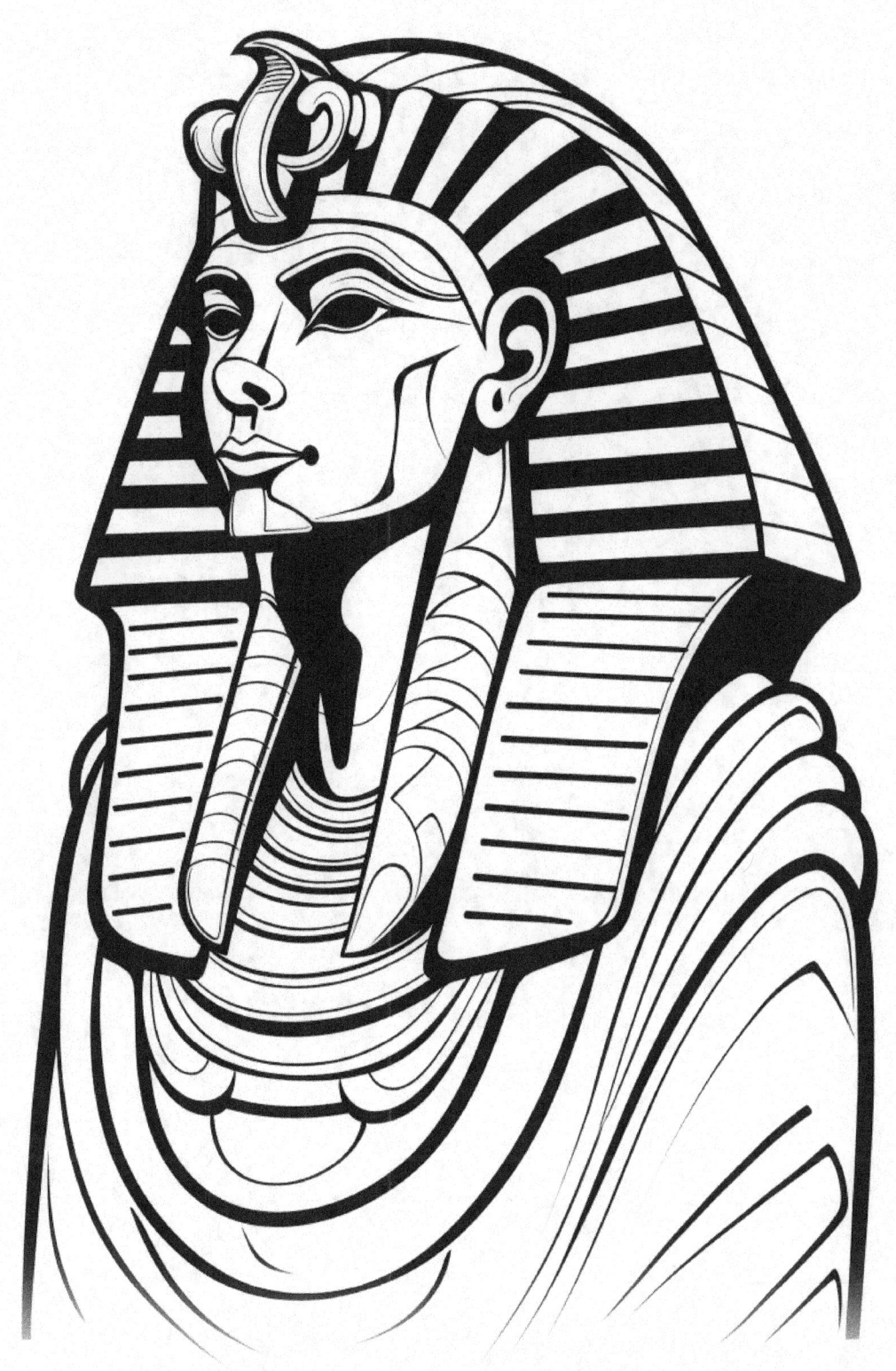

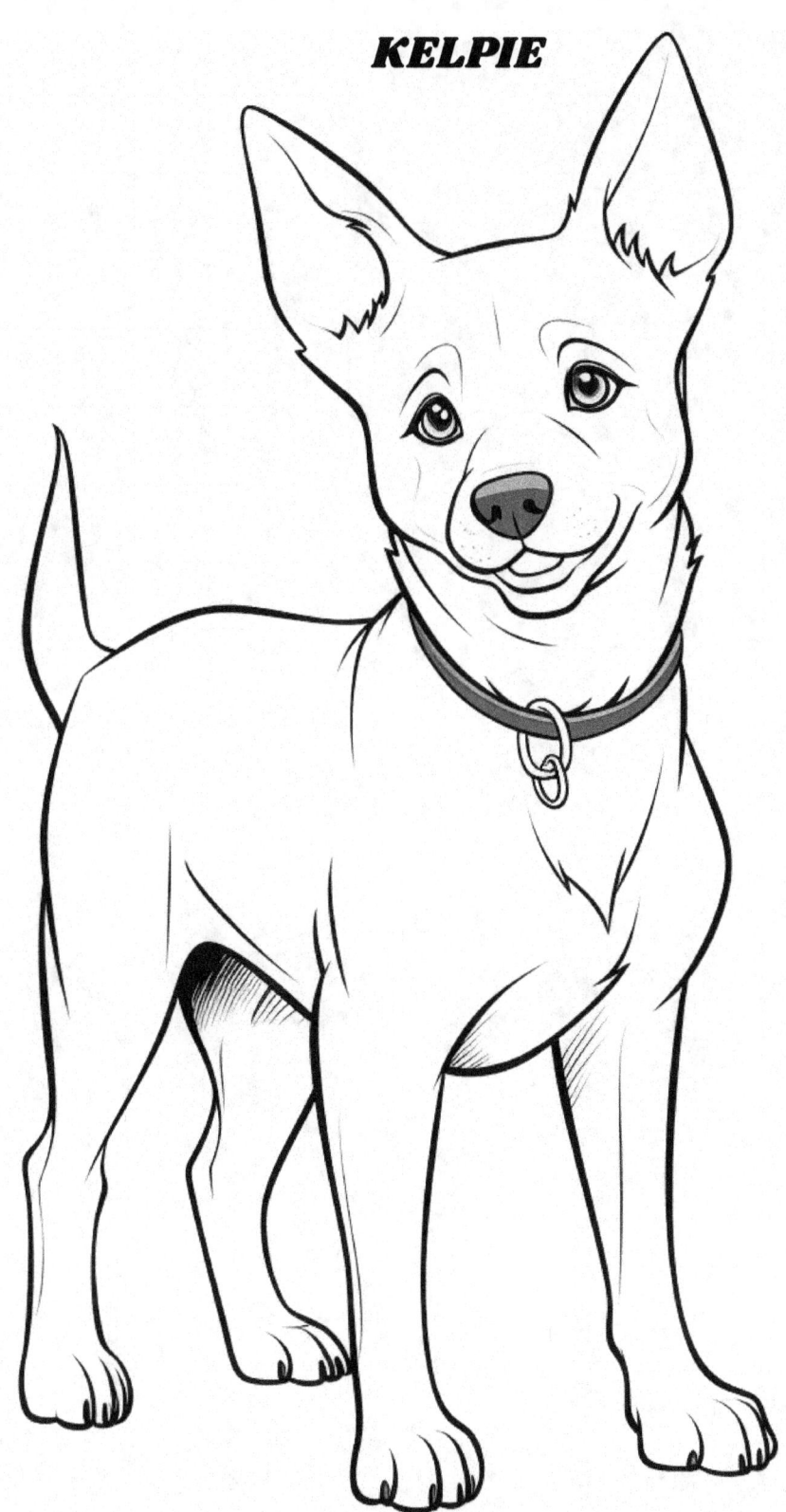

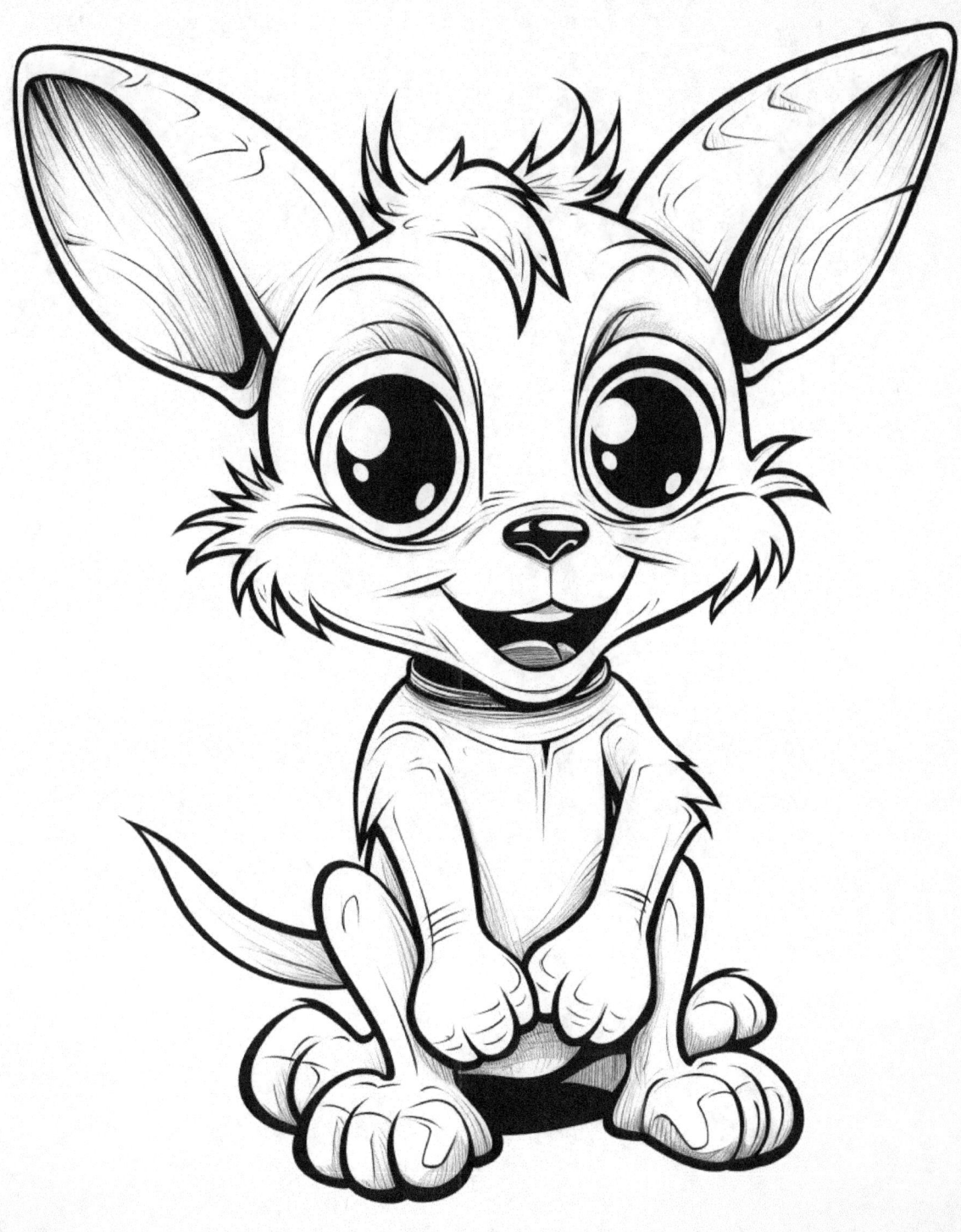

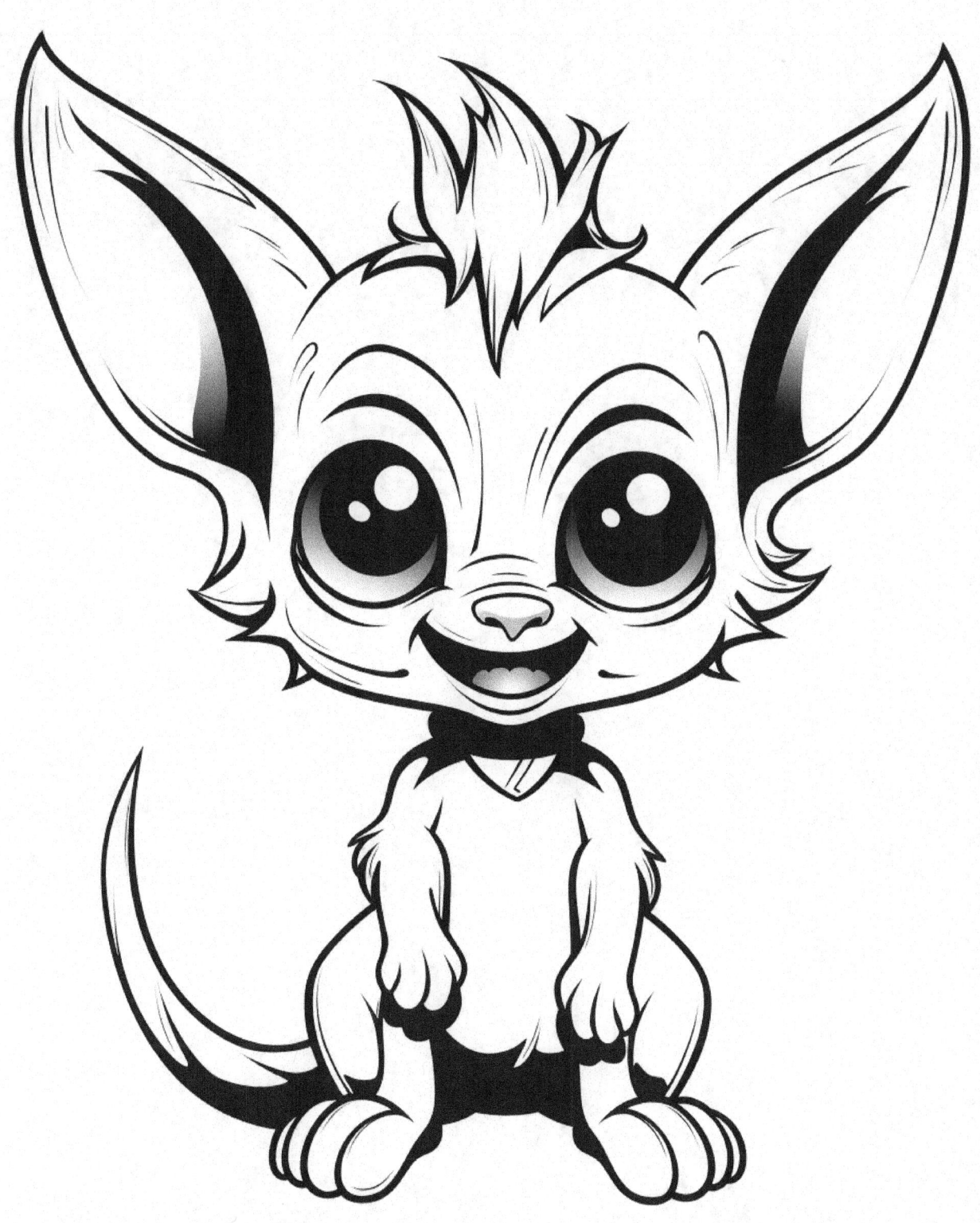

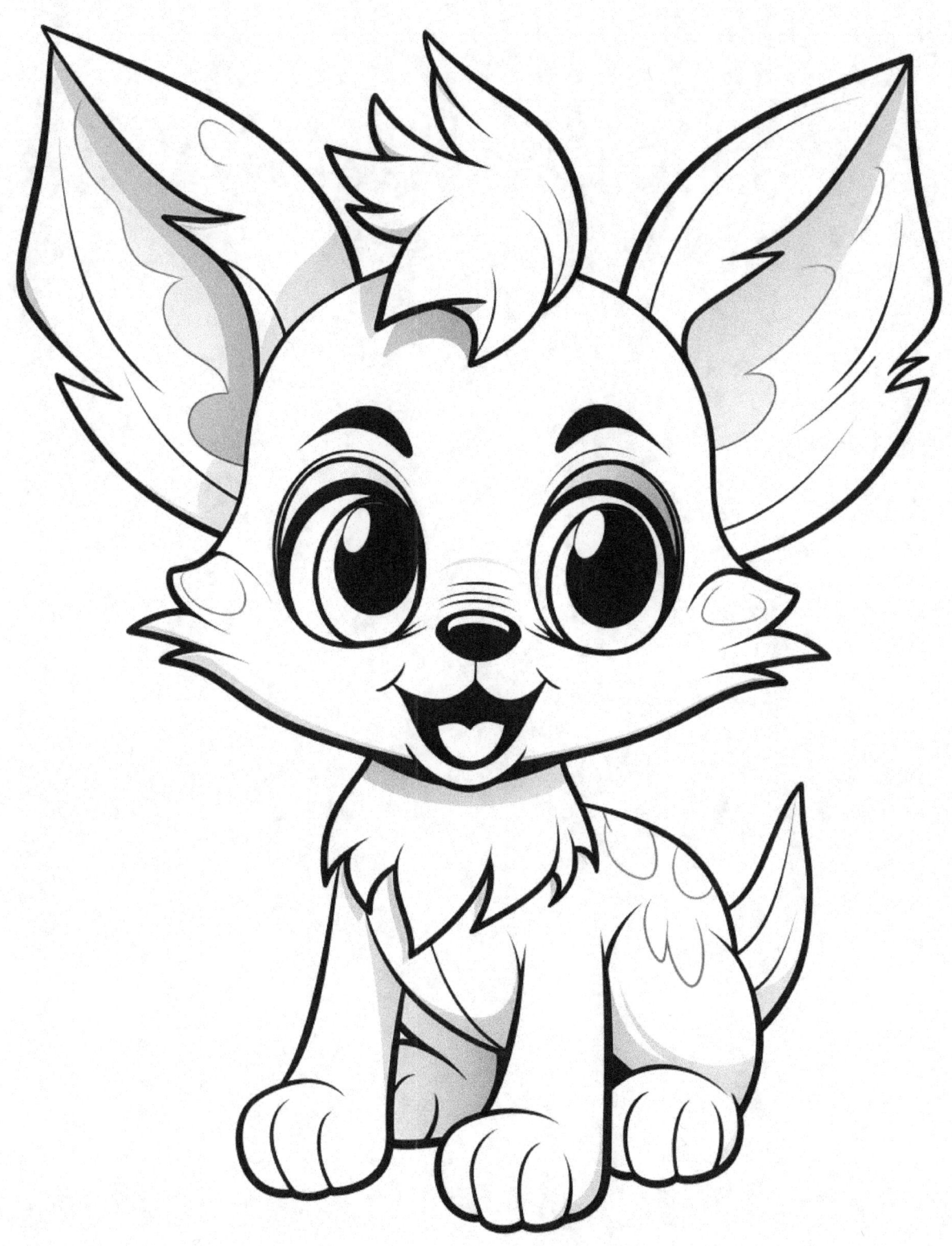

NAGA

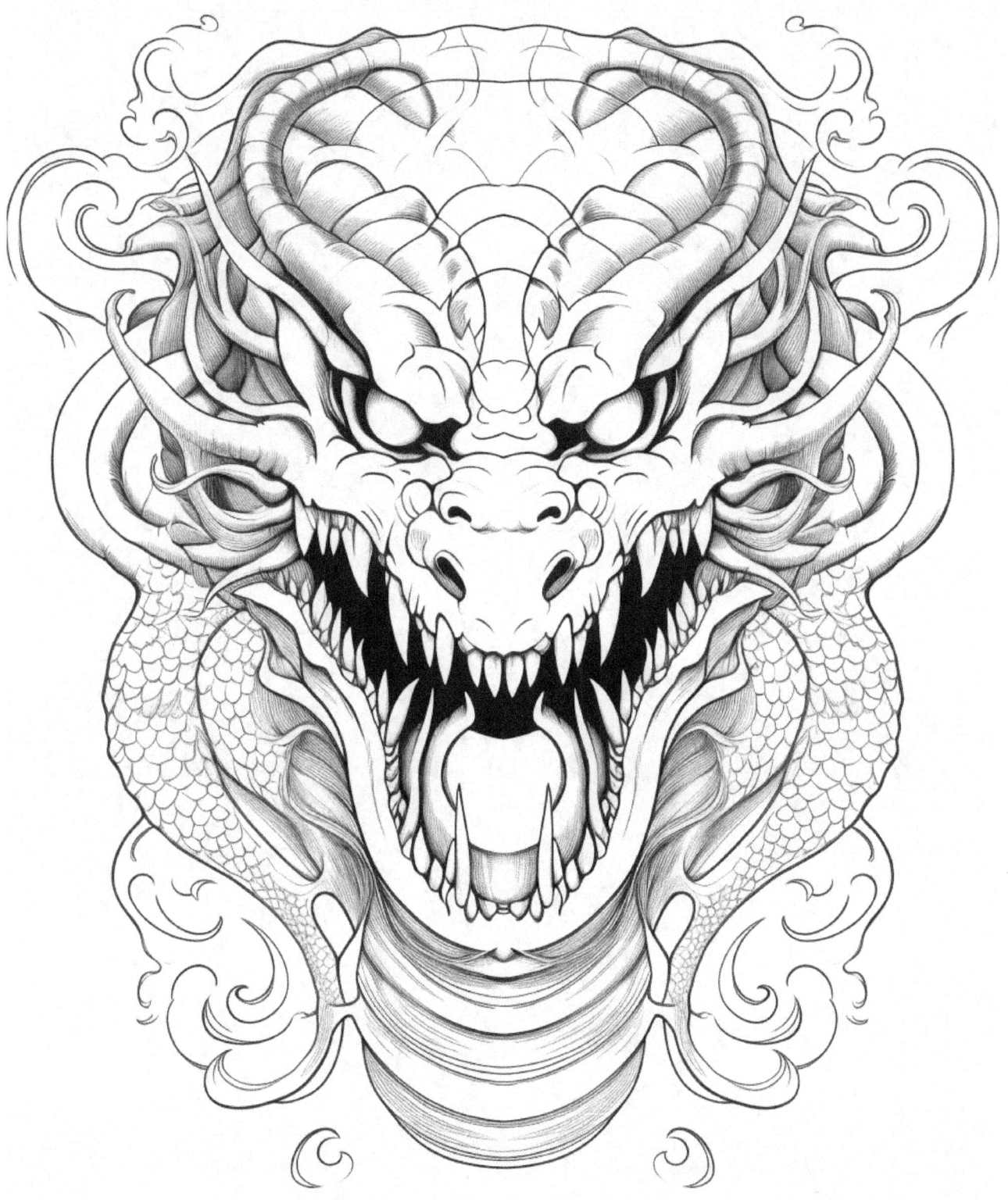

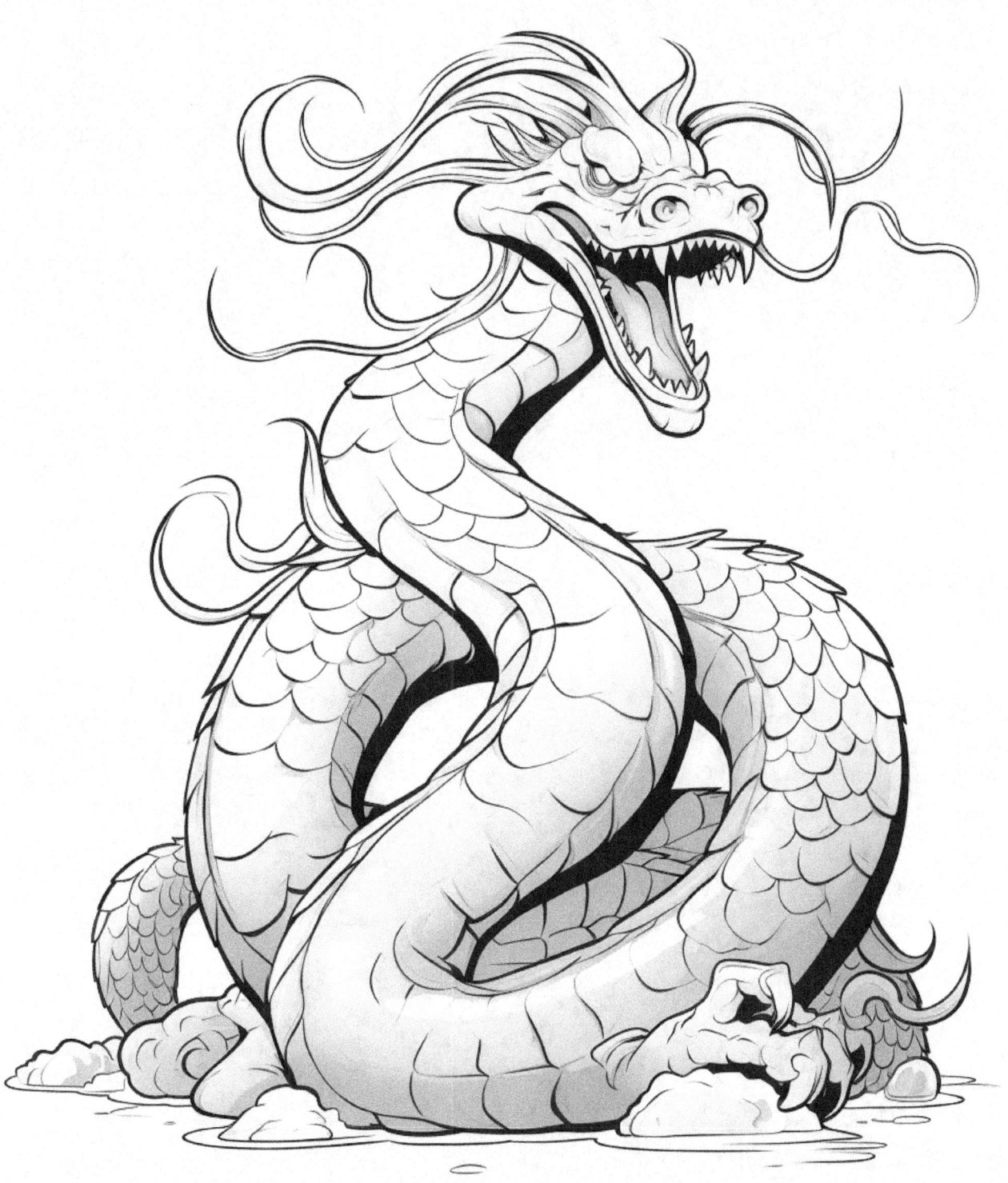

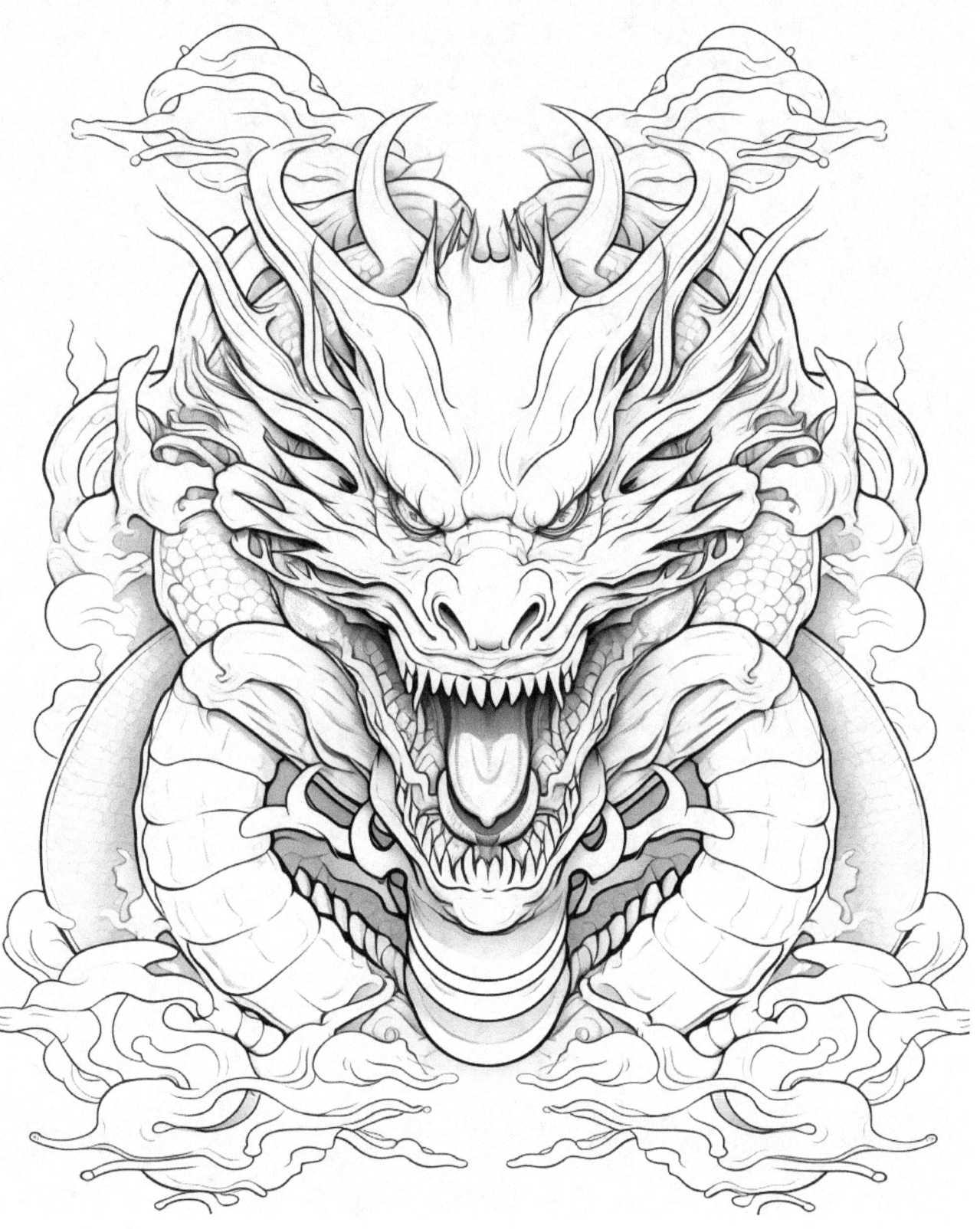

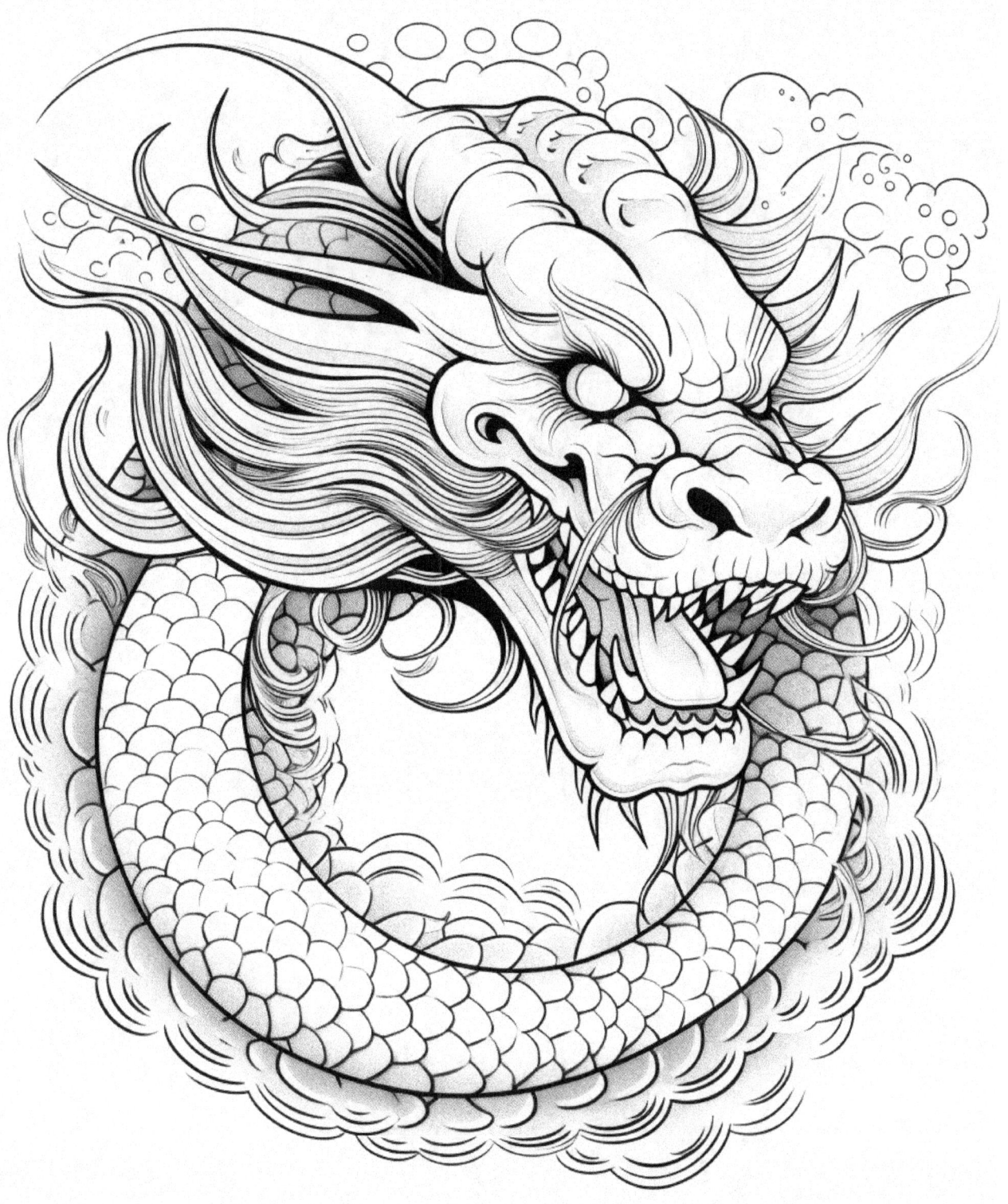

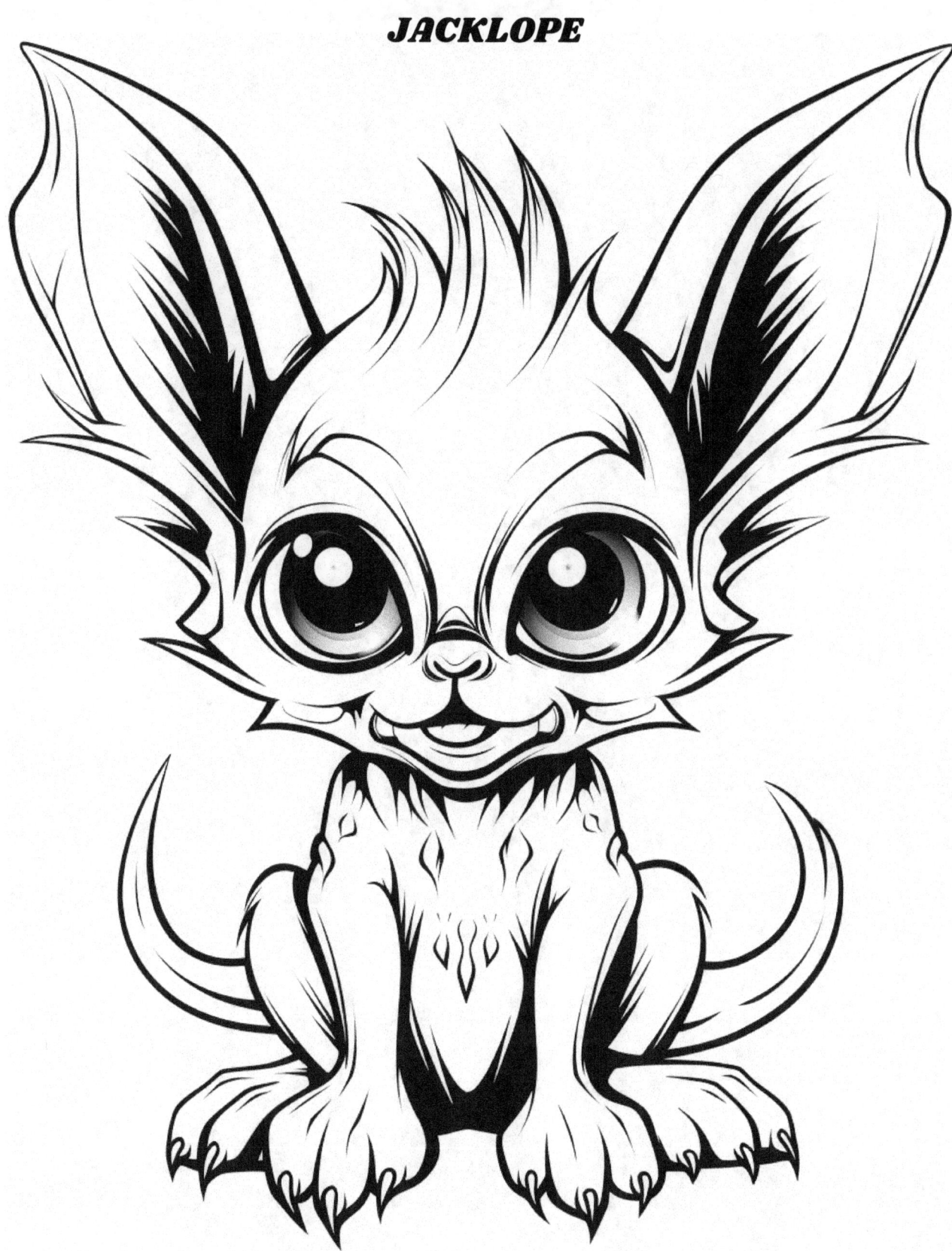

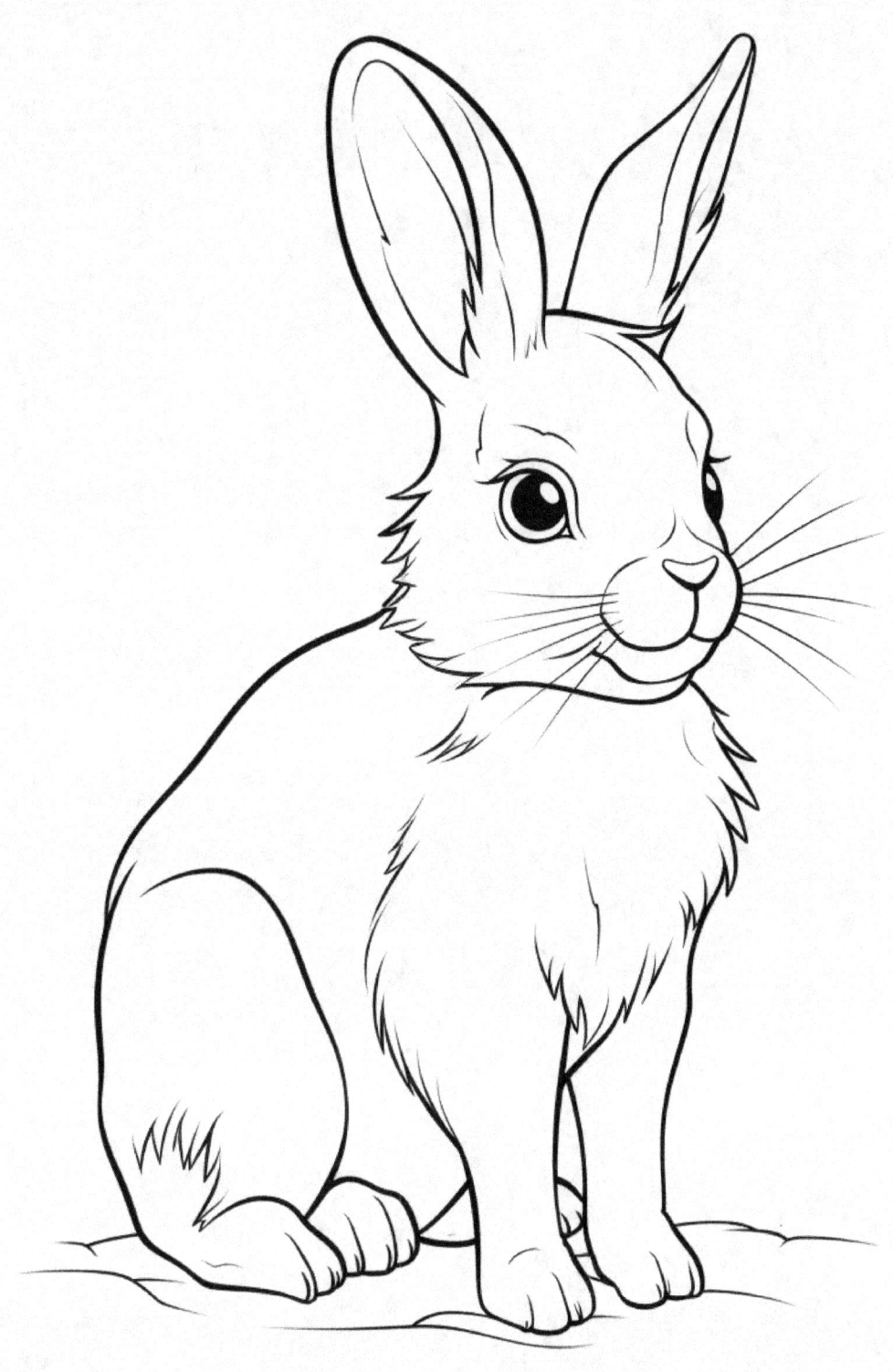

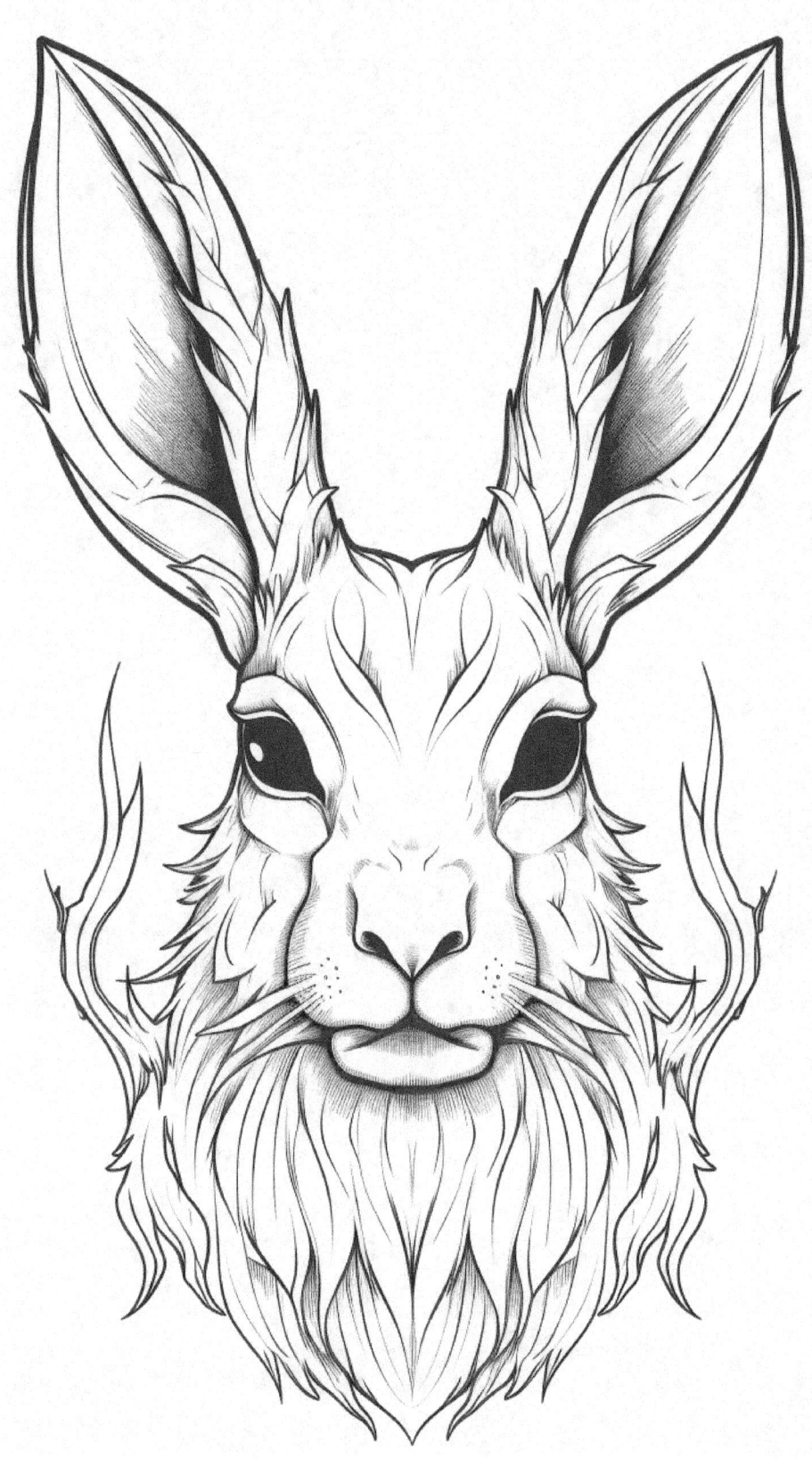

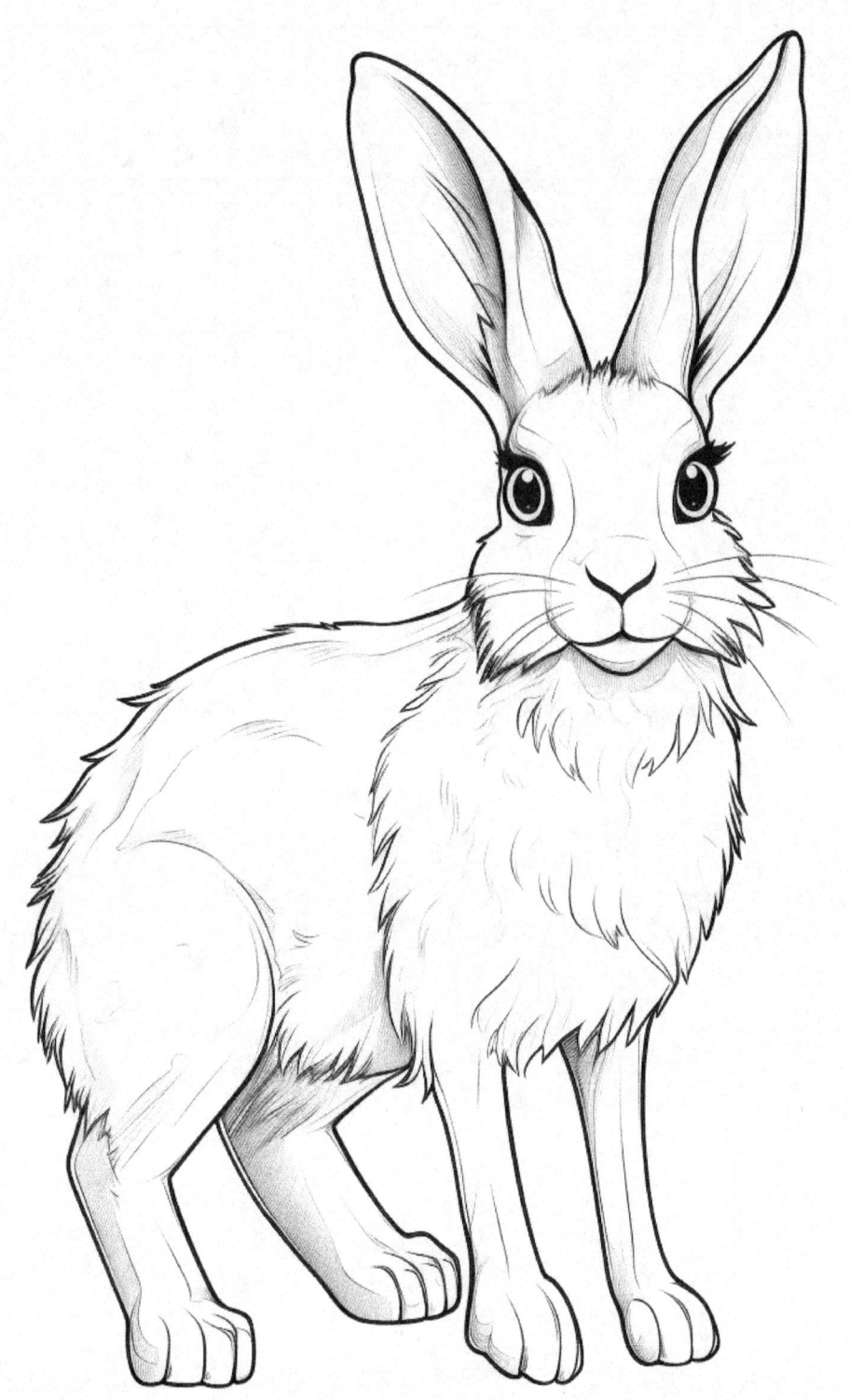

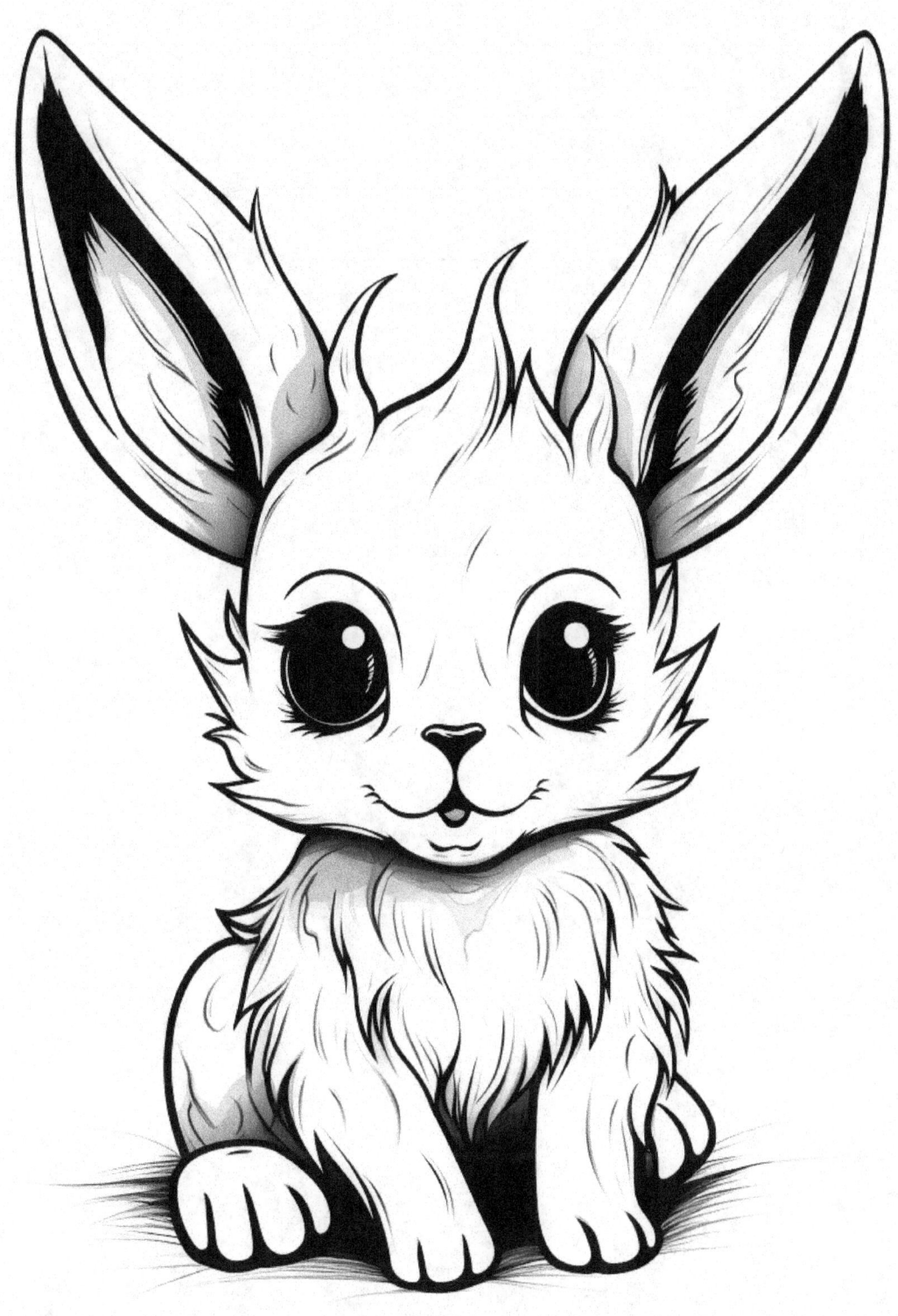

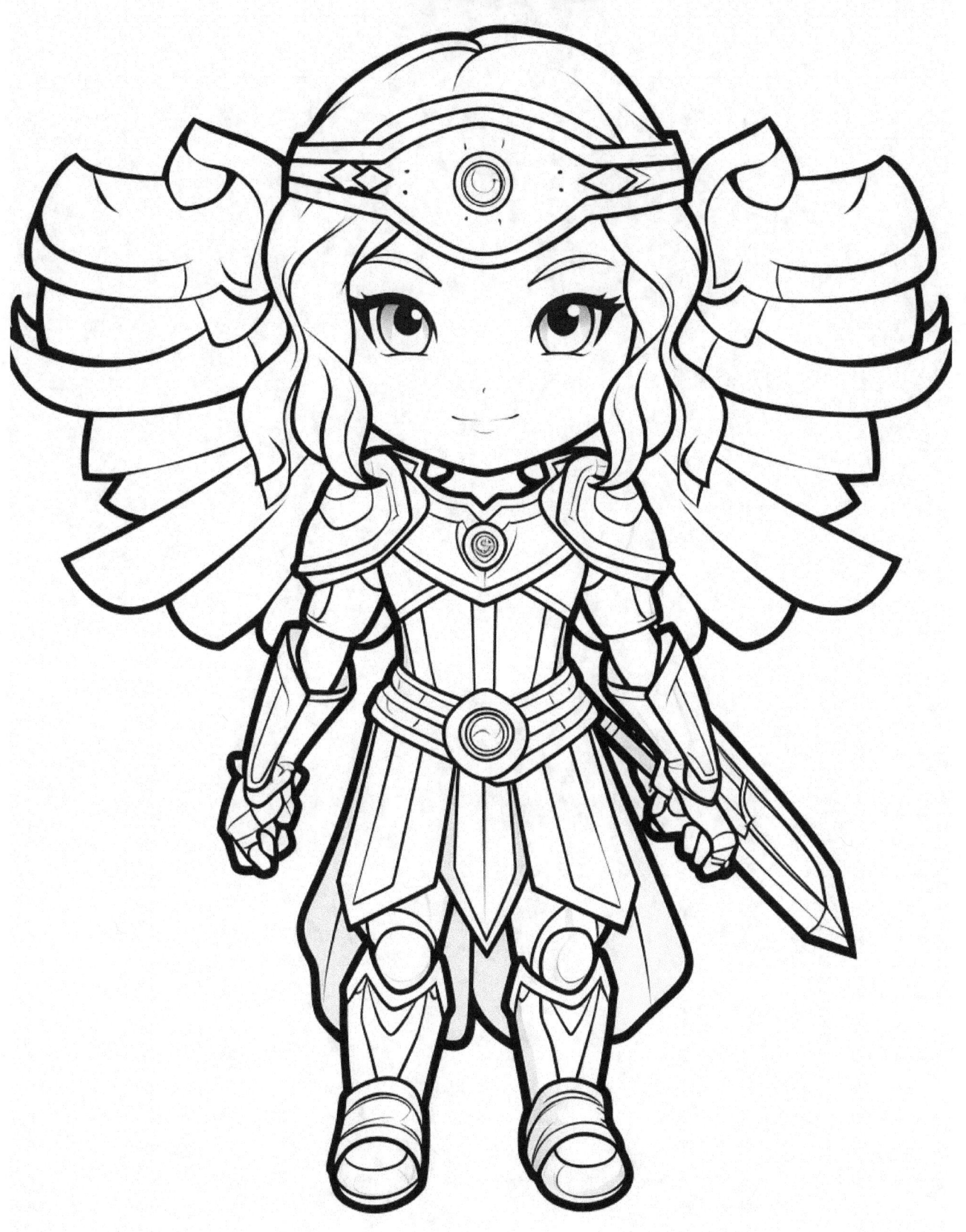

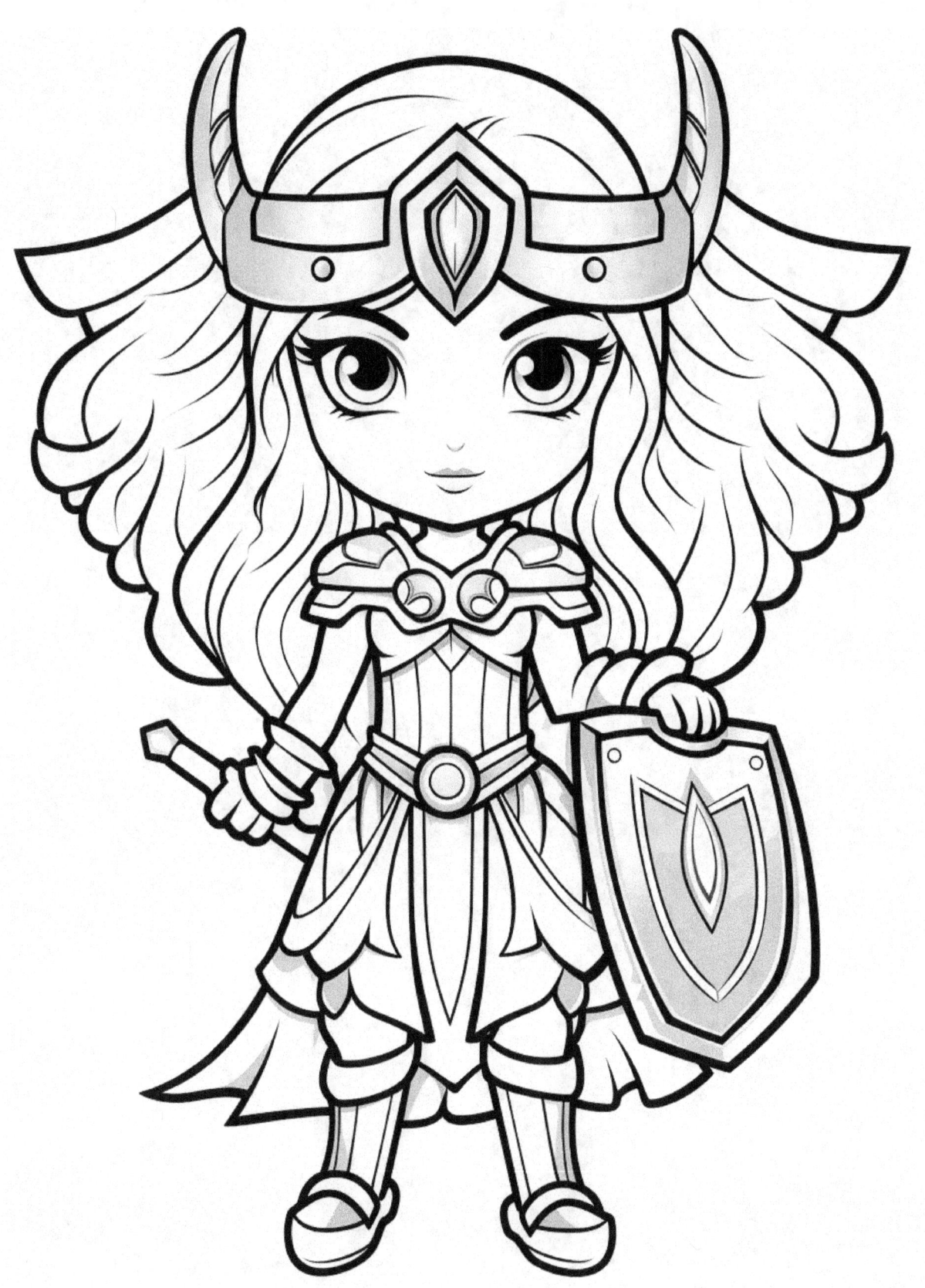

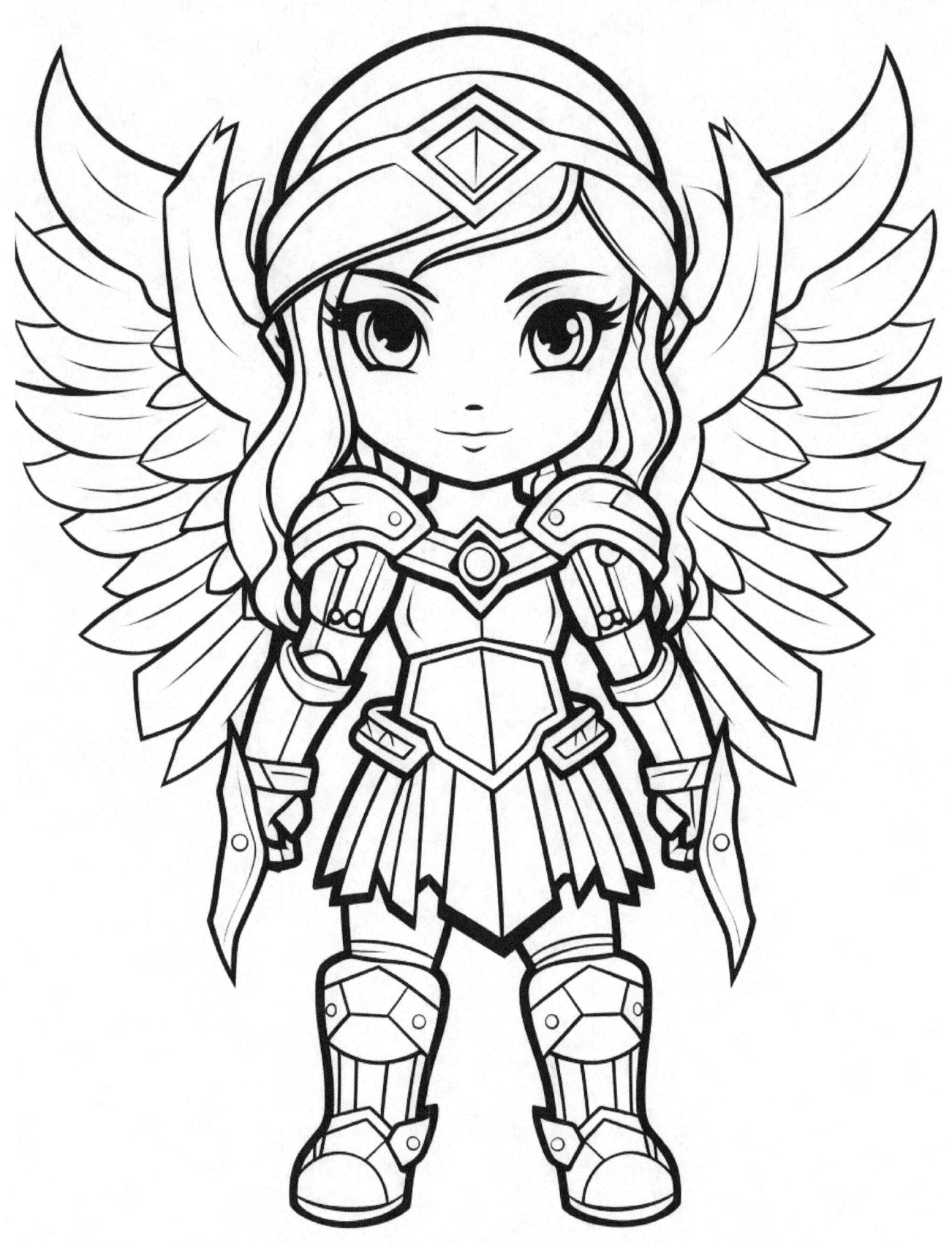

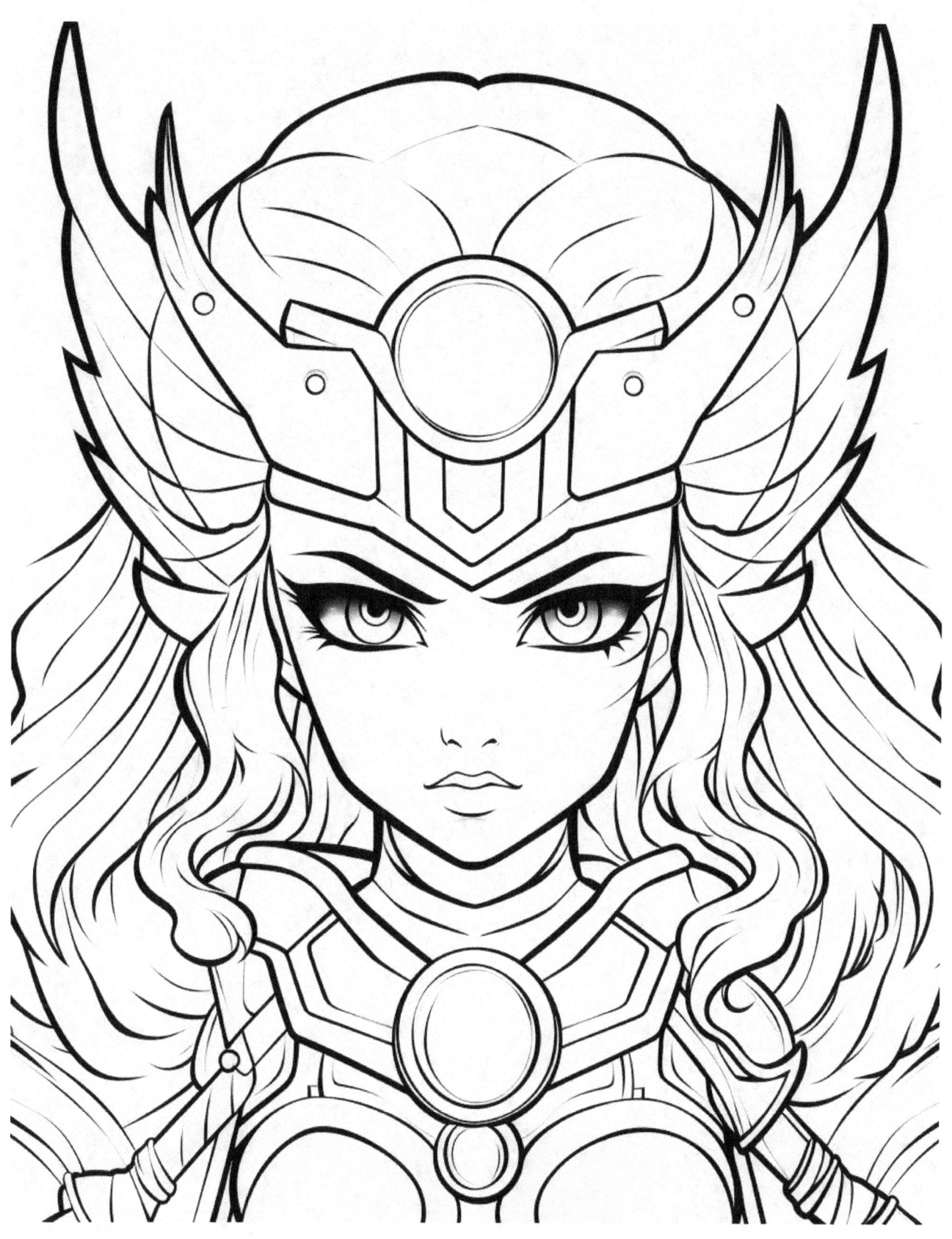

LEPRECHAUN

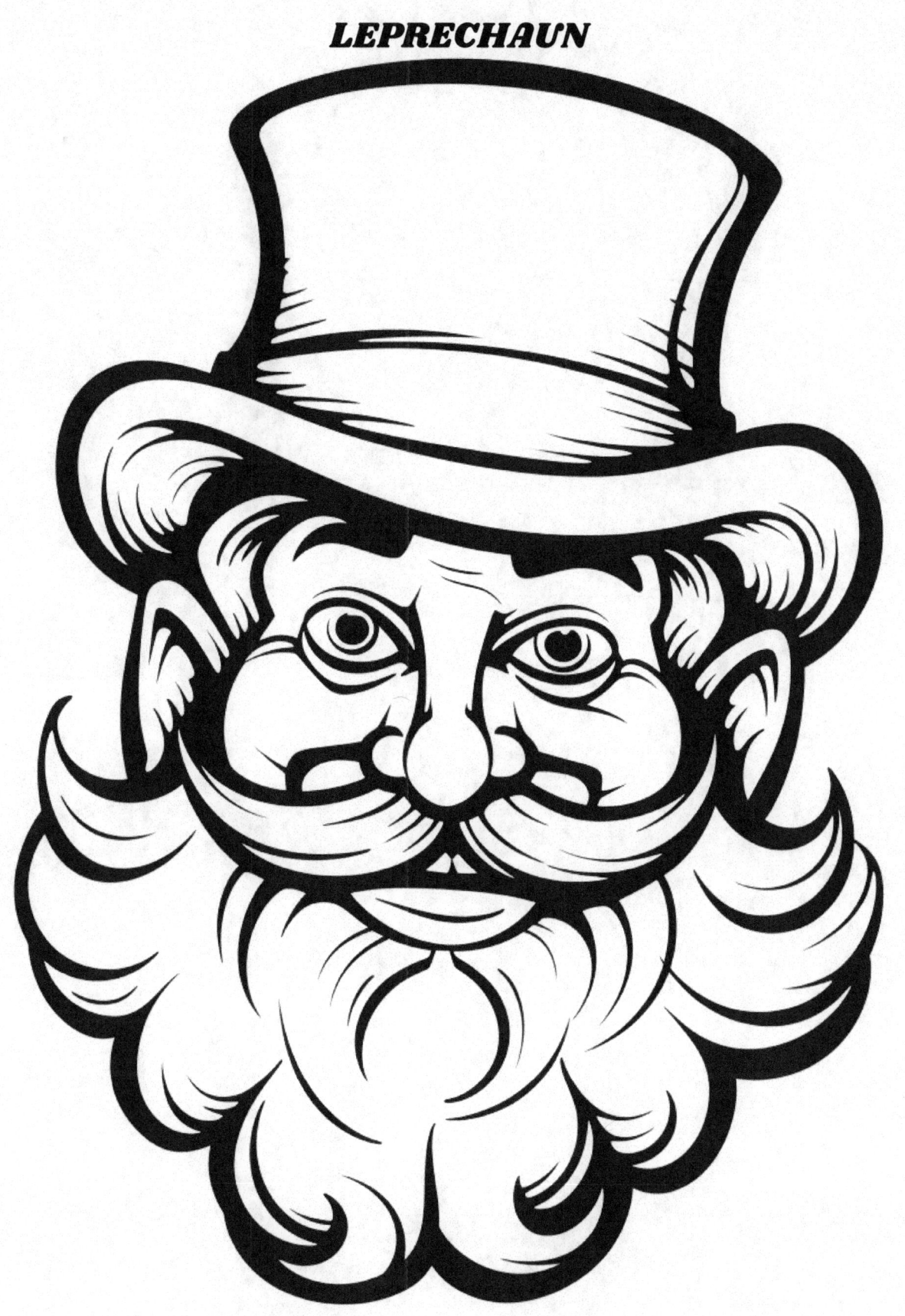

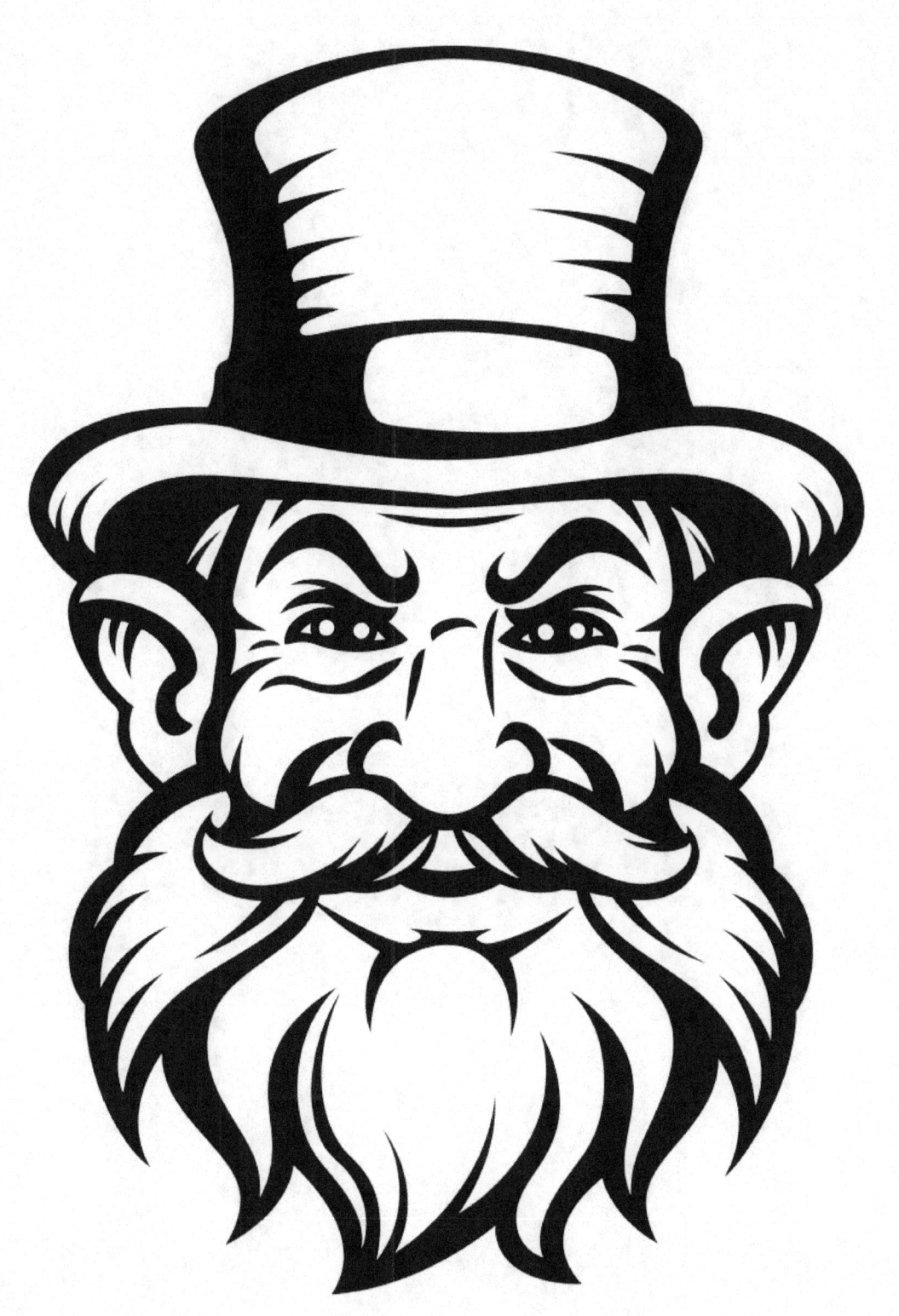

GNOME

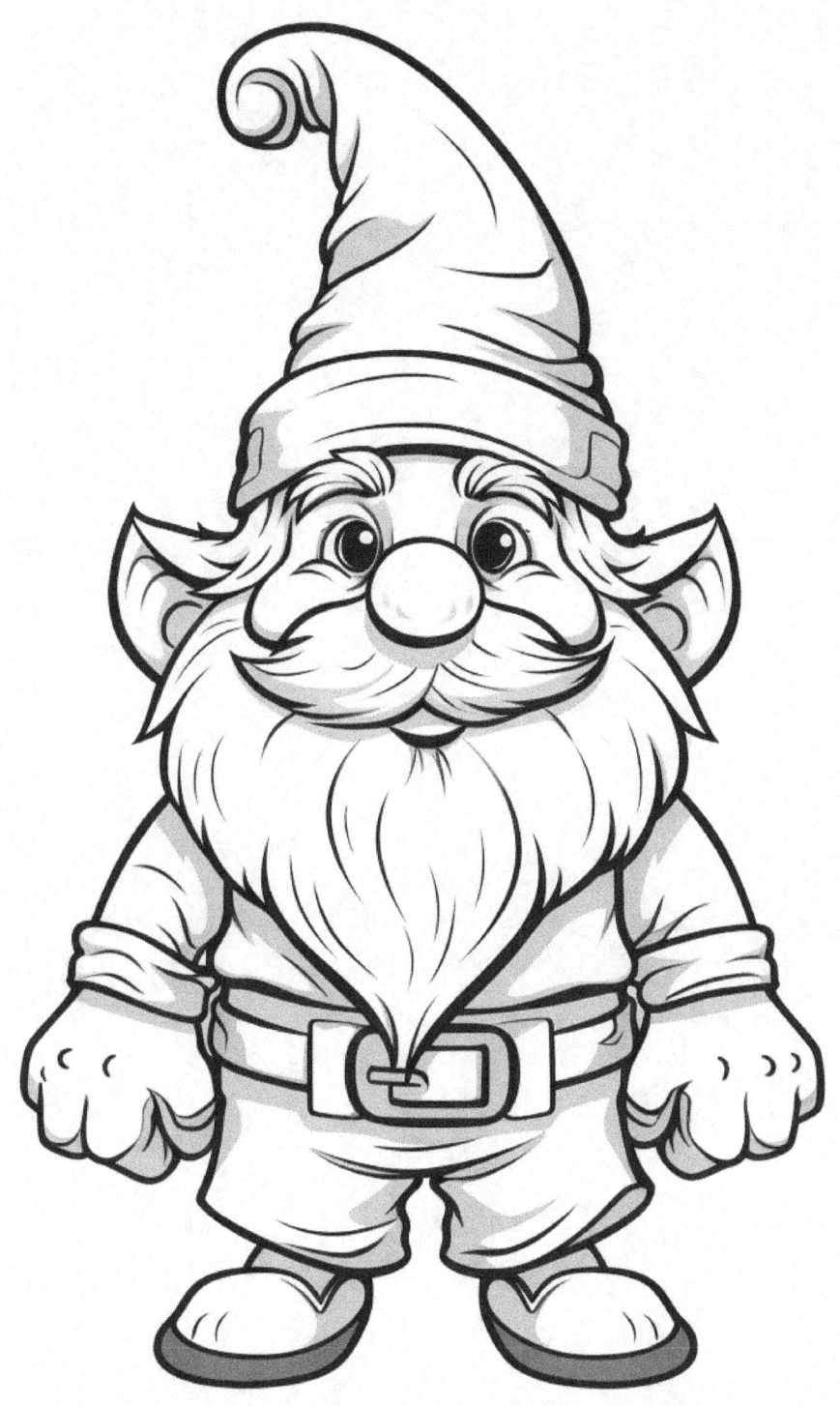

THUNDERBIRD

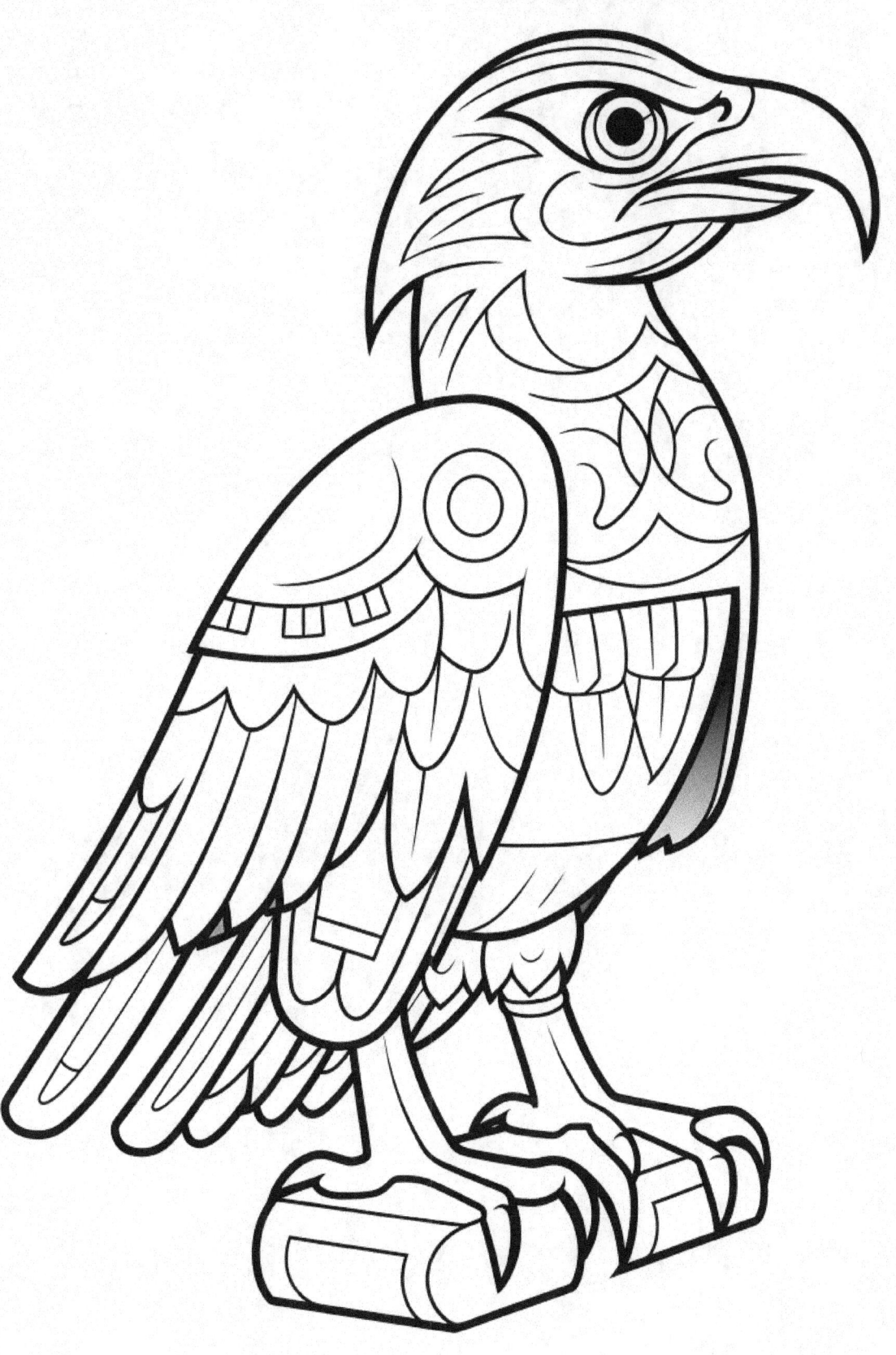

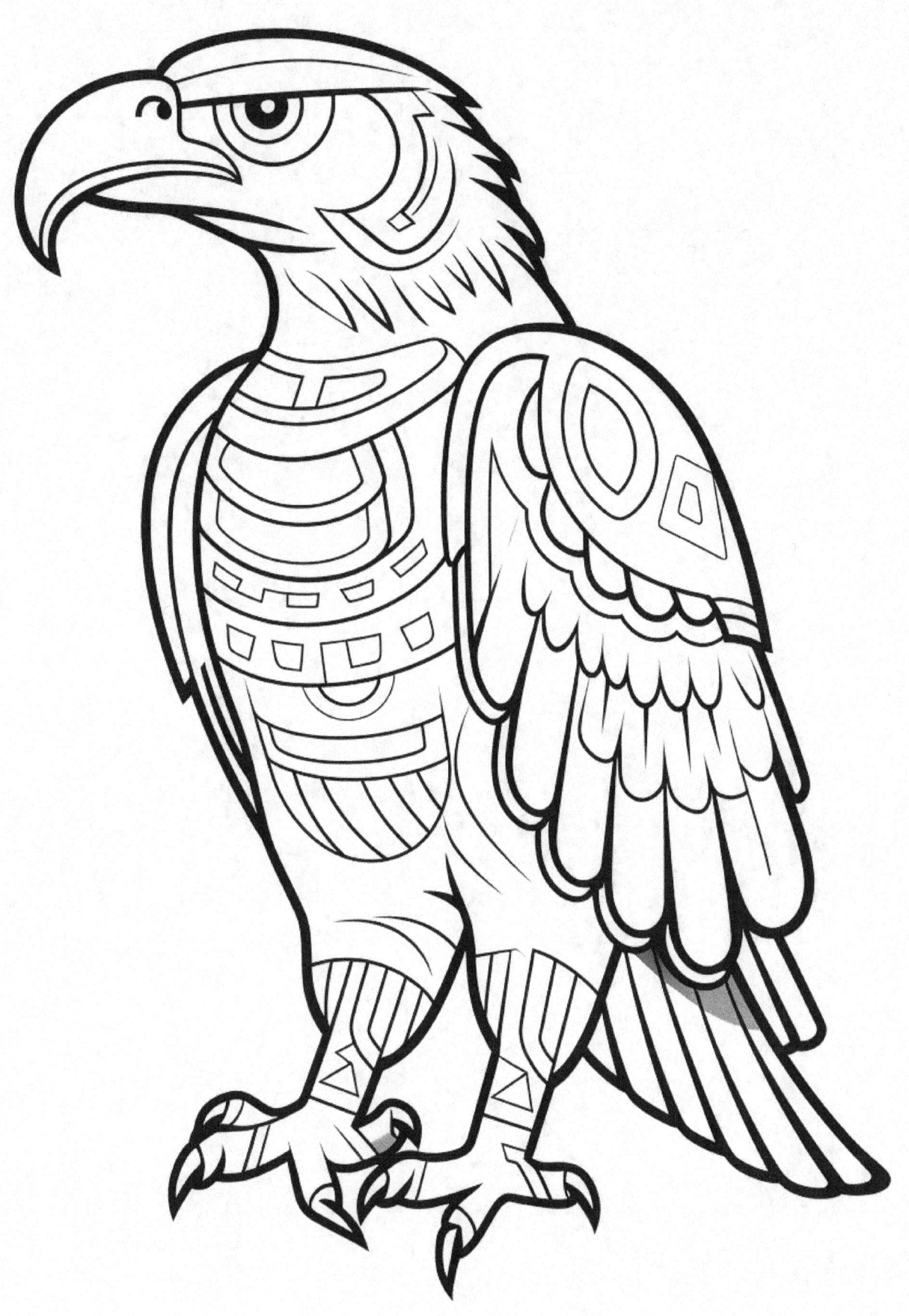

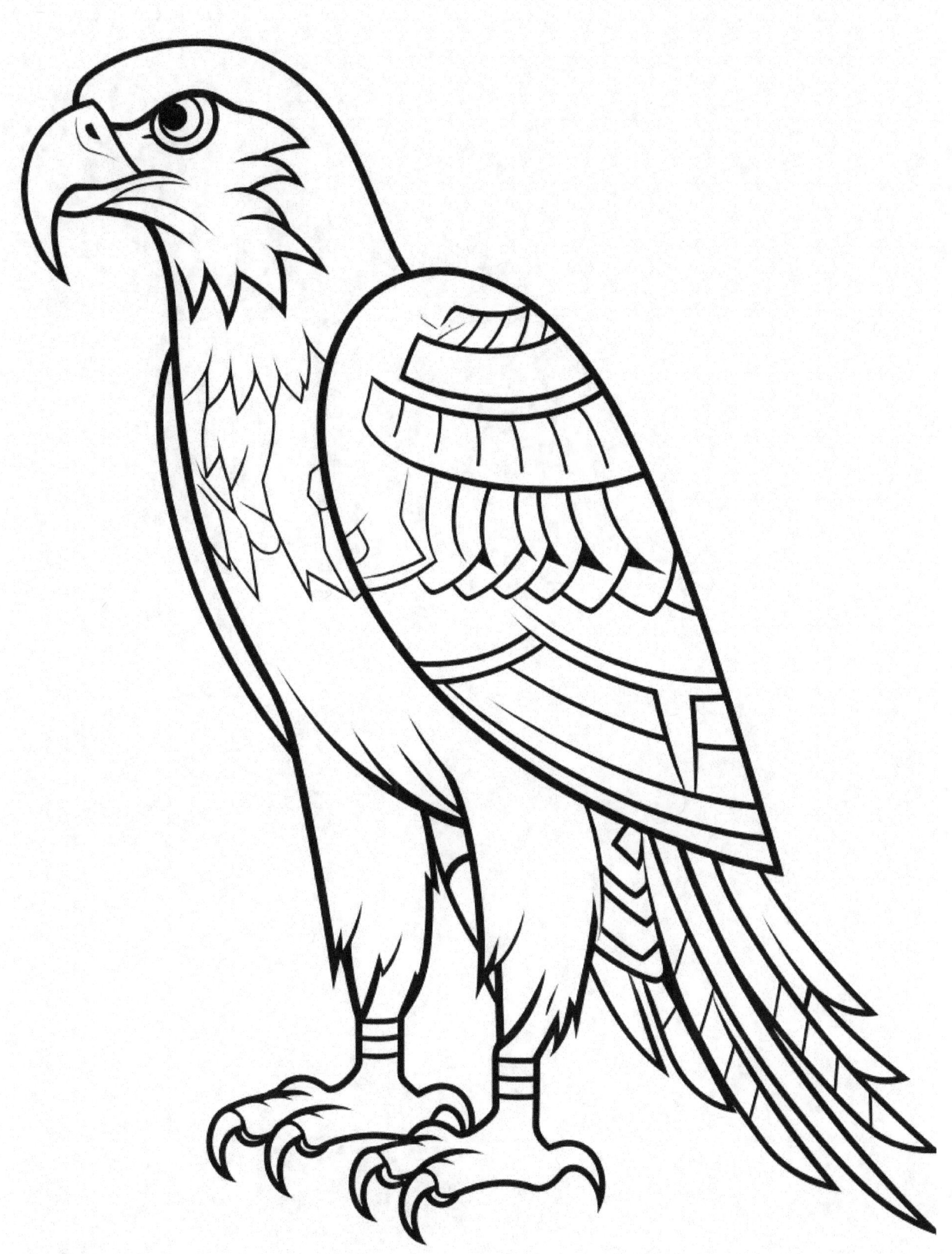

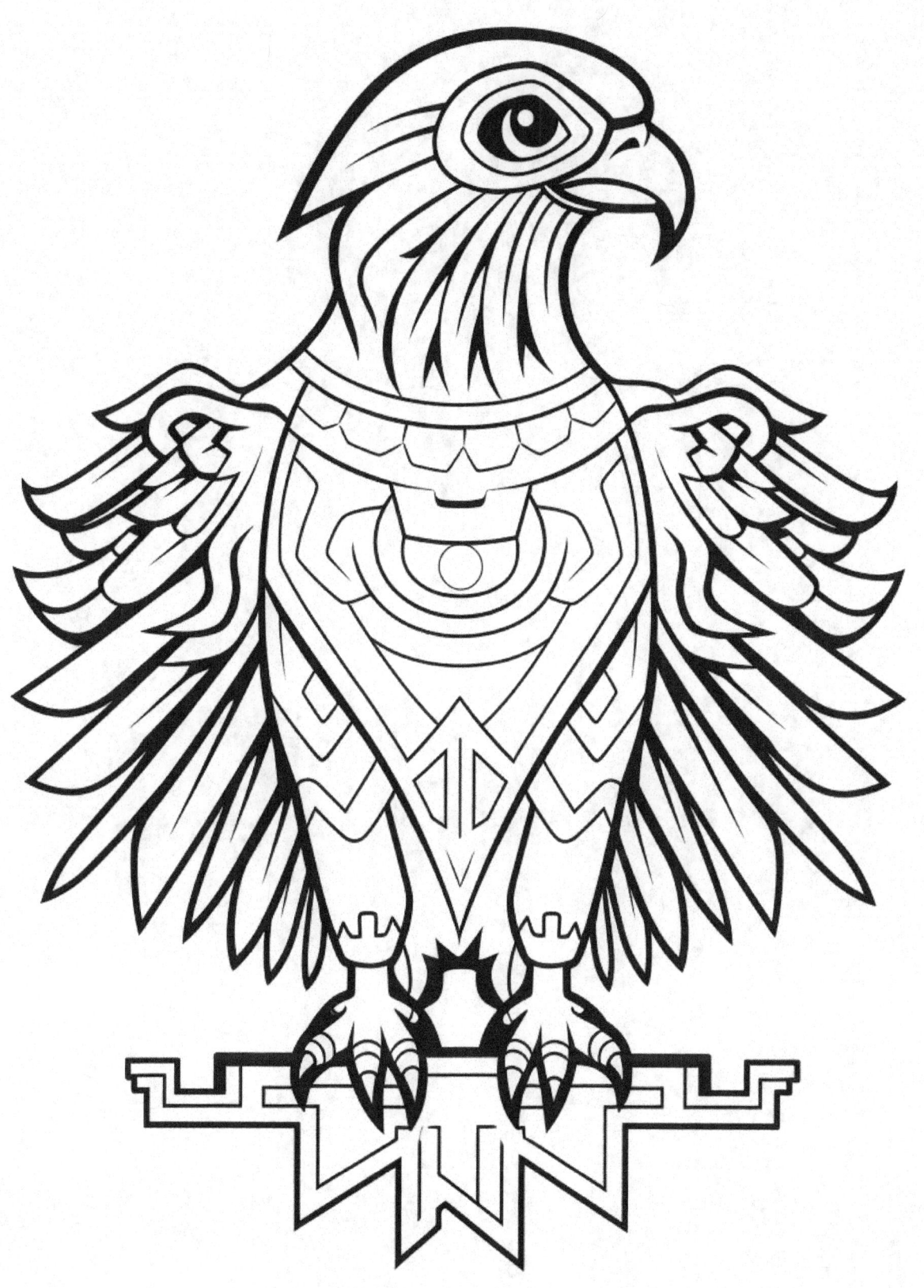

HIPPO GRIEF

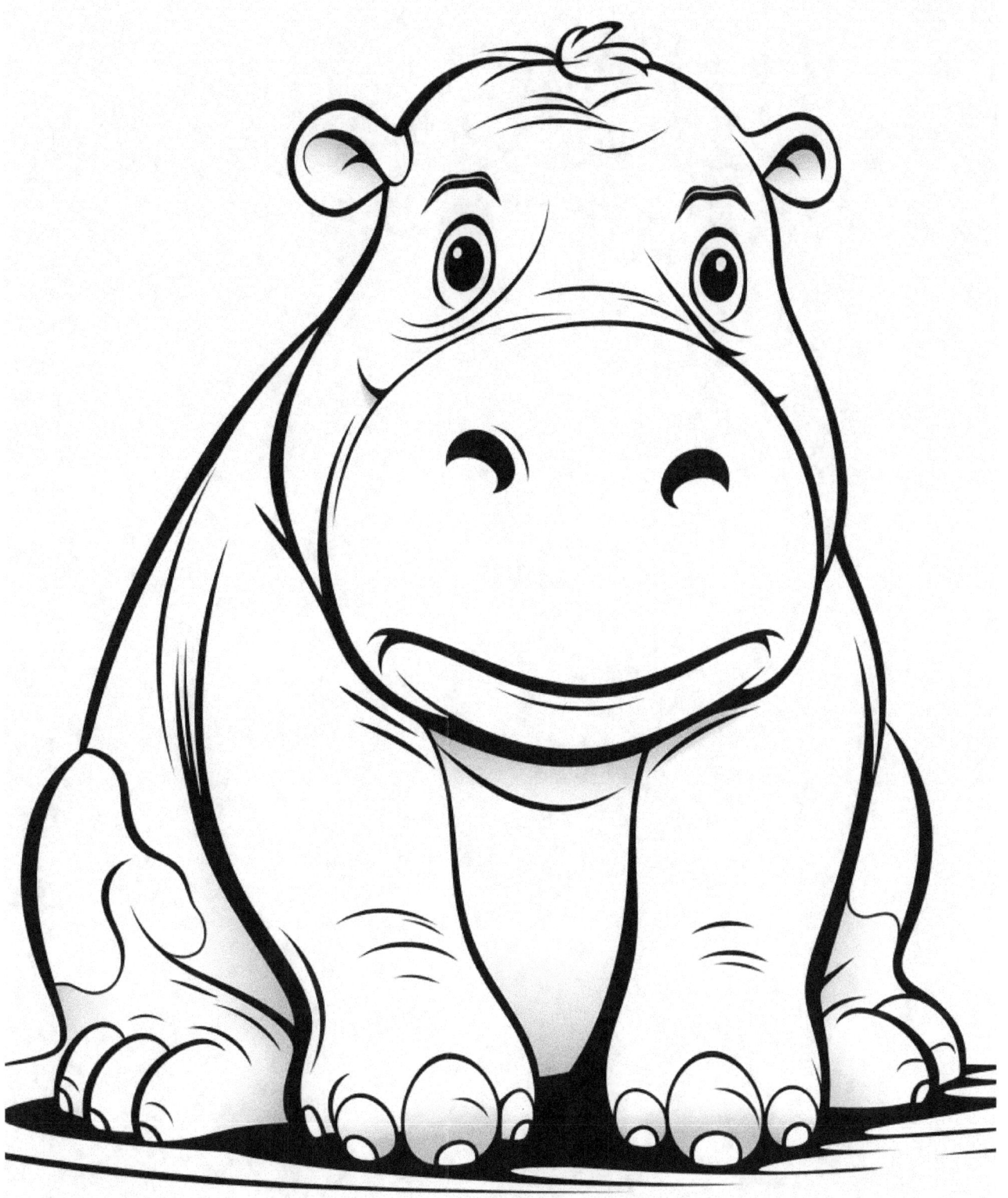

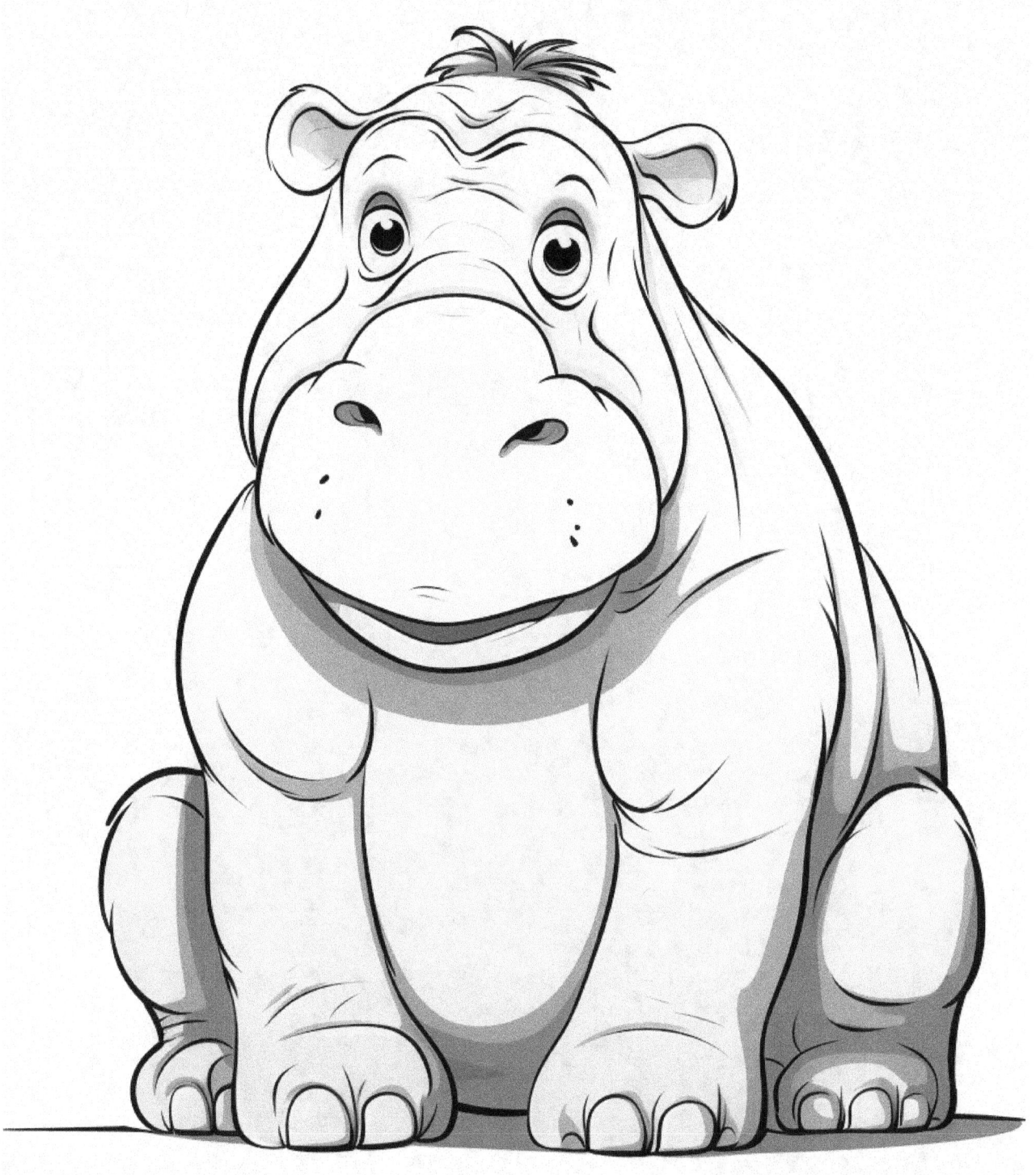

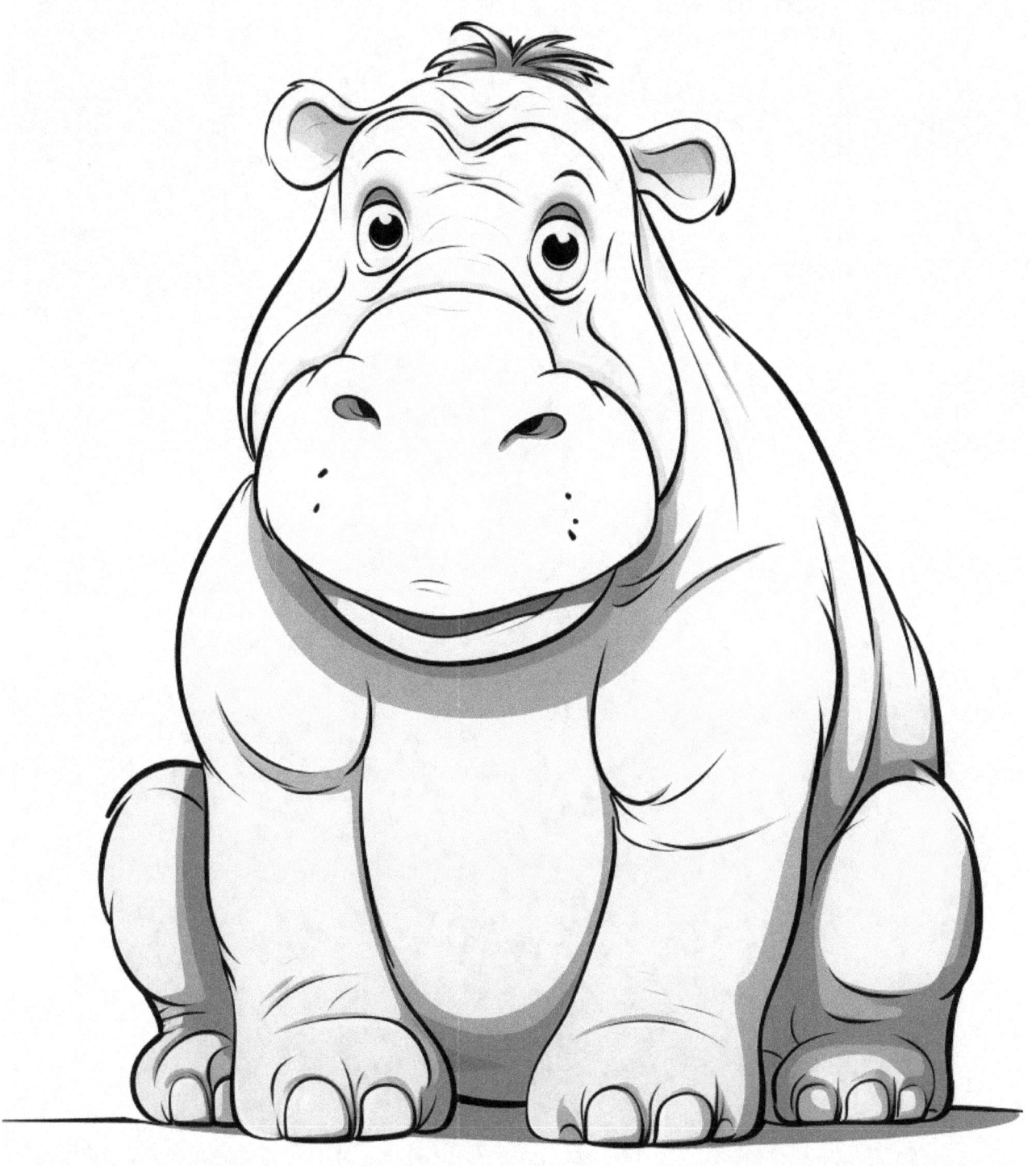

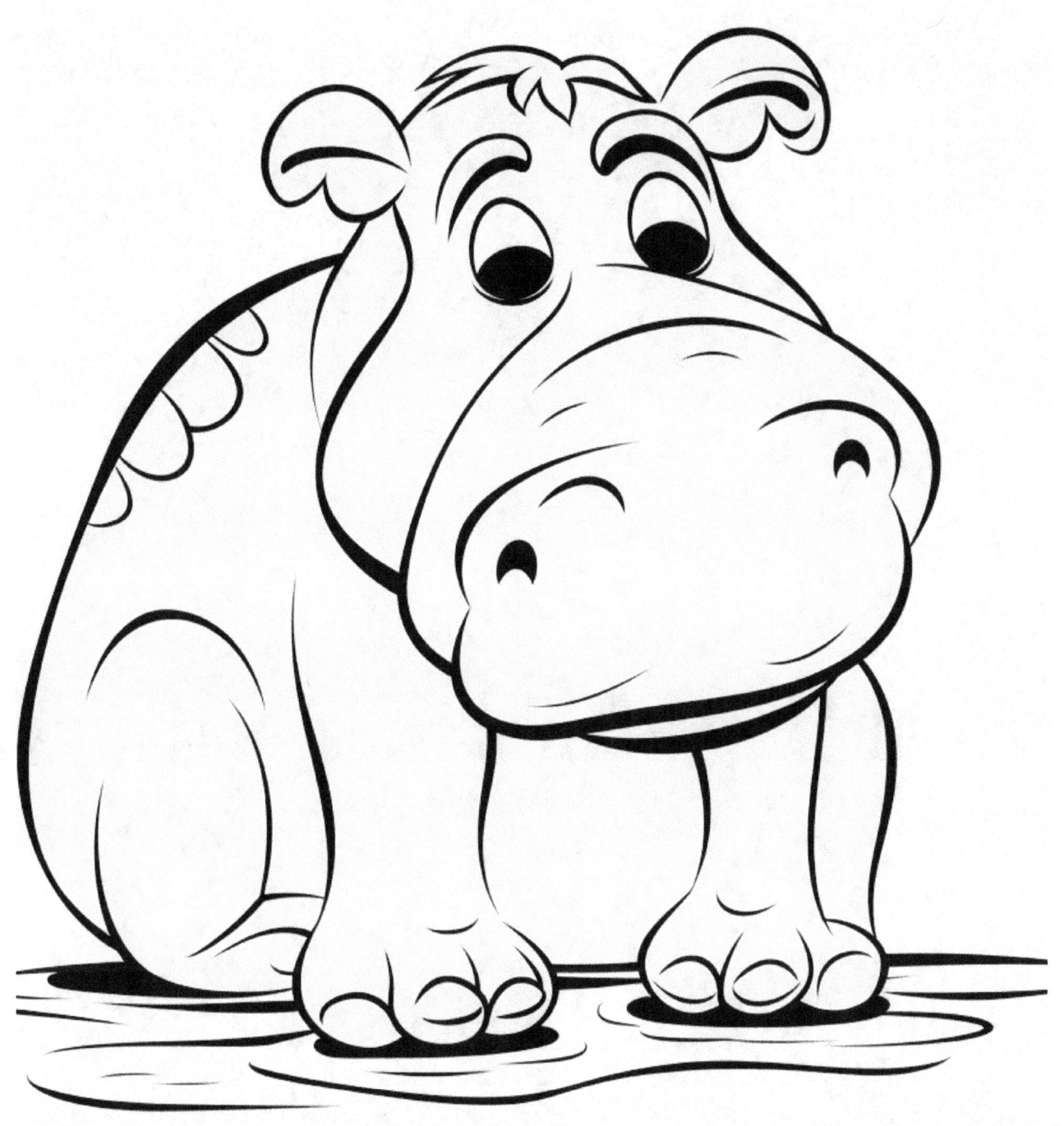

KITSUNE

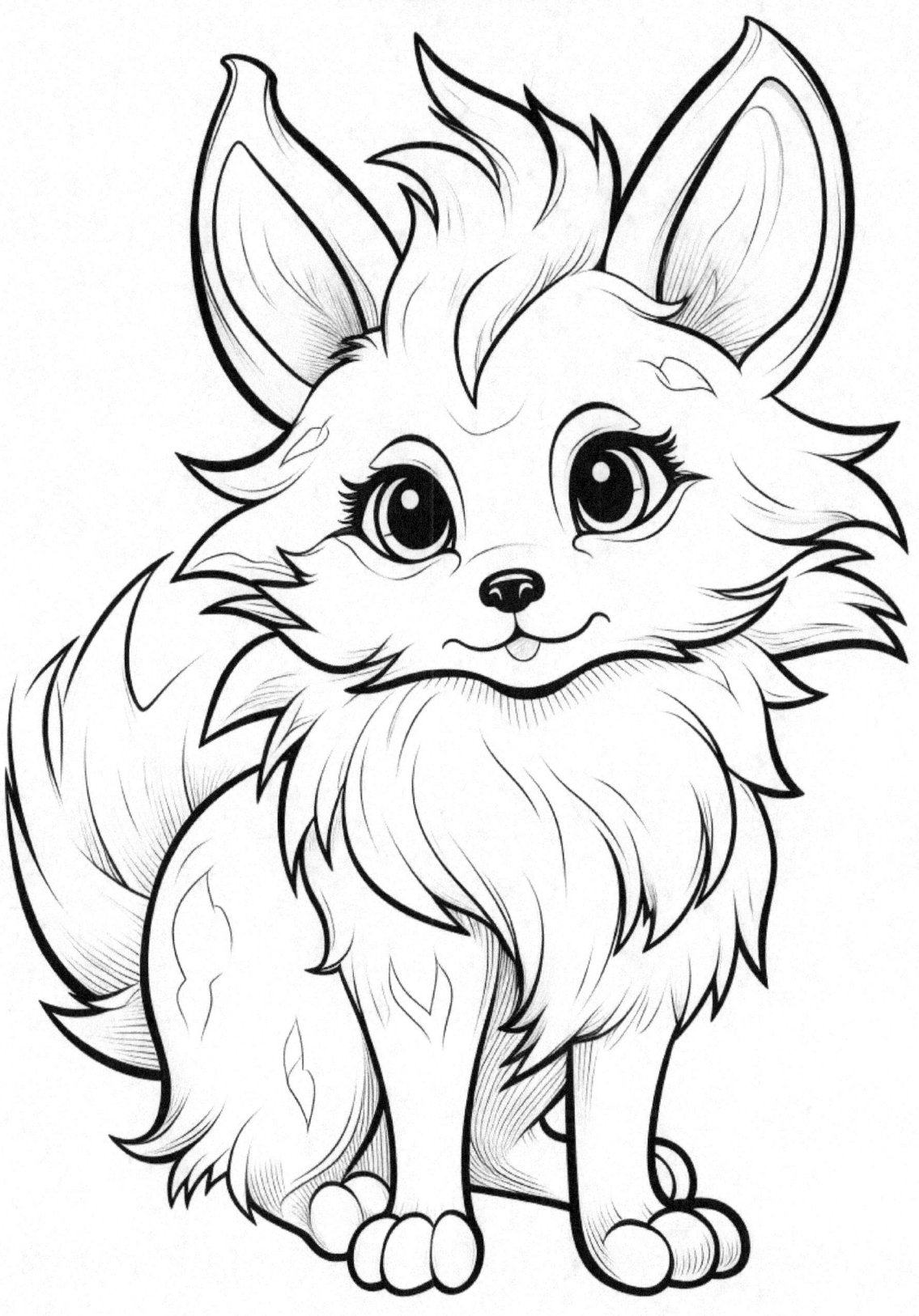

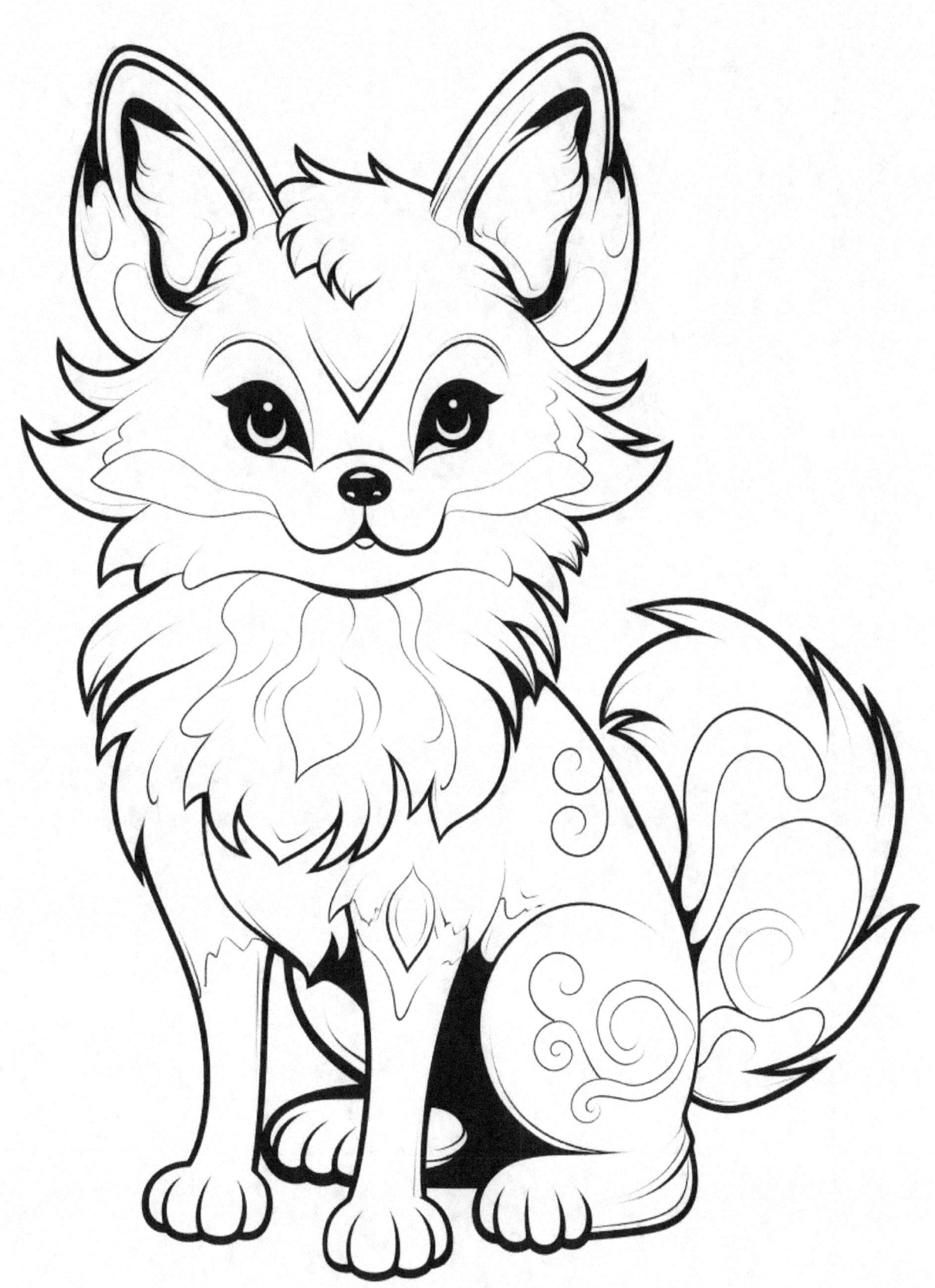

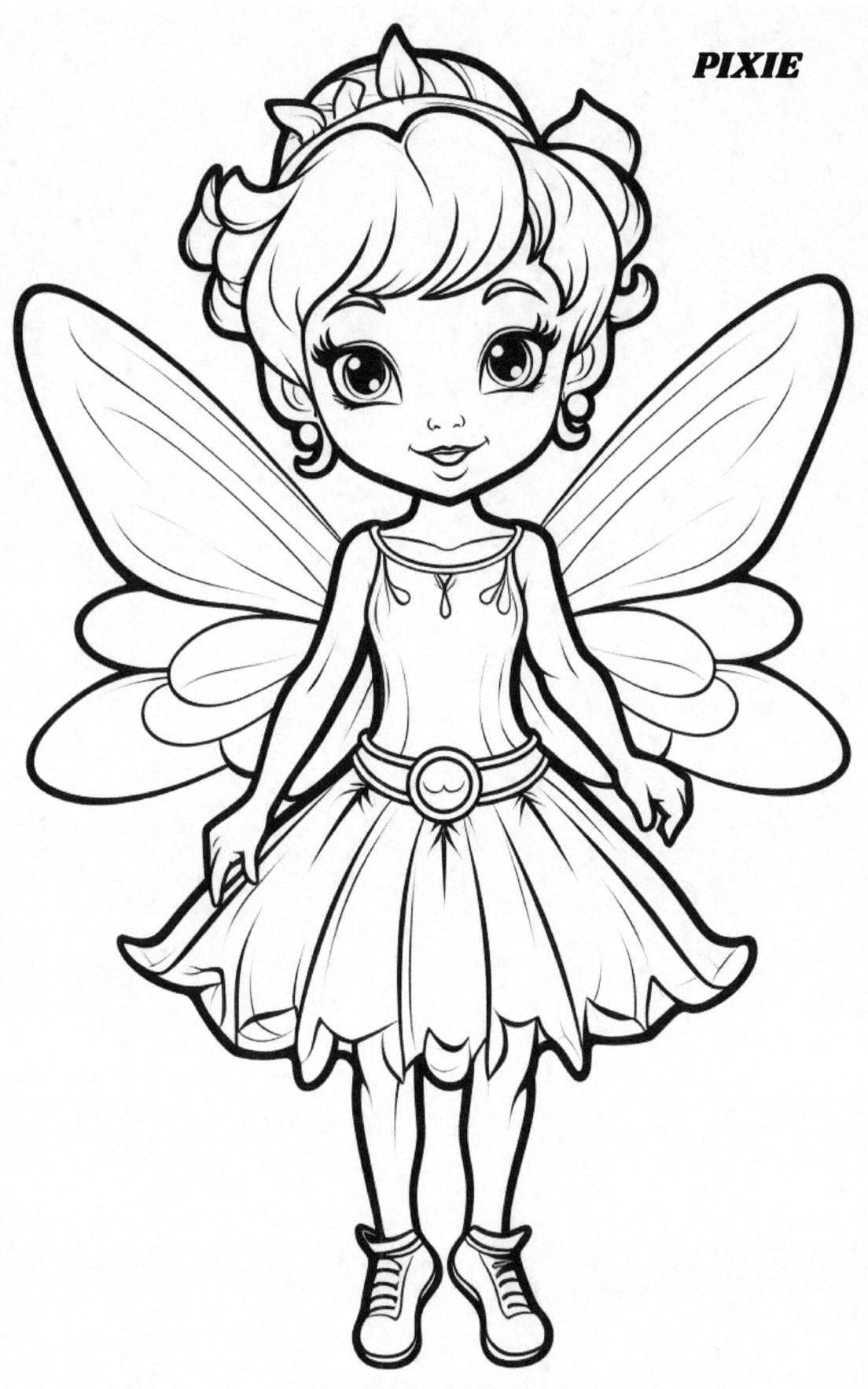

PIXIE

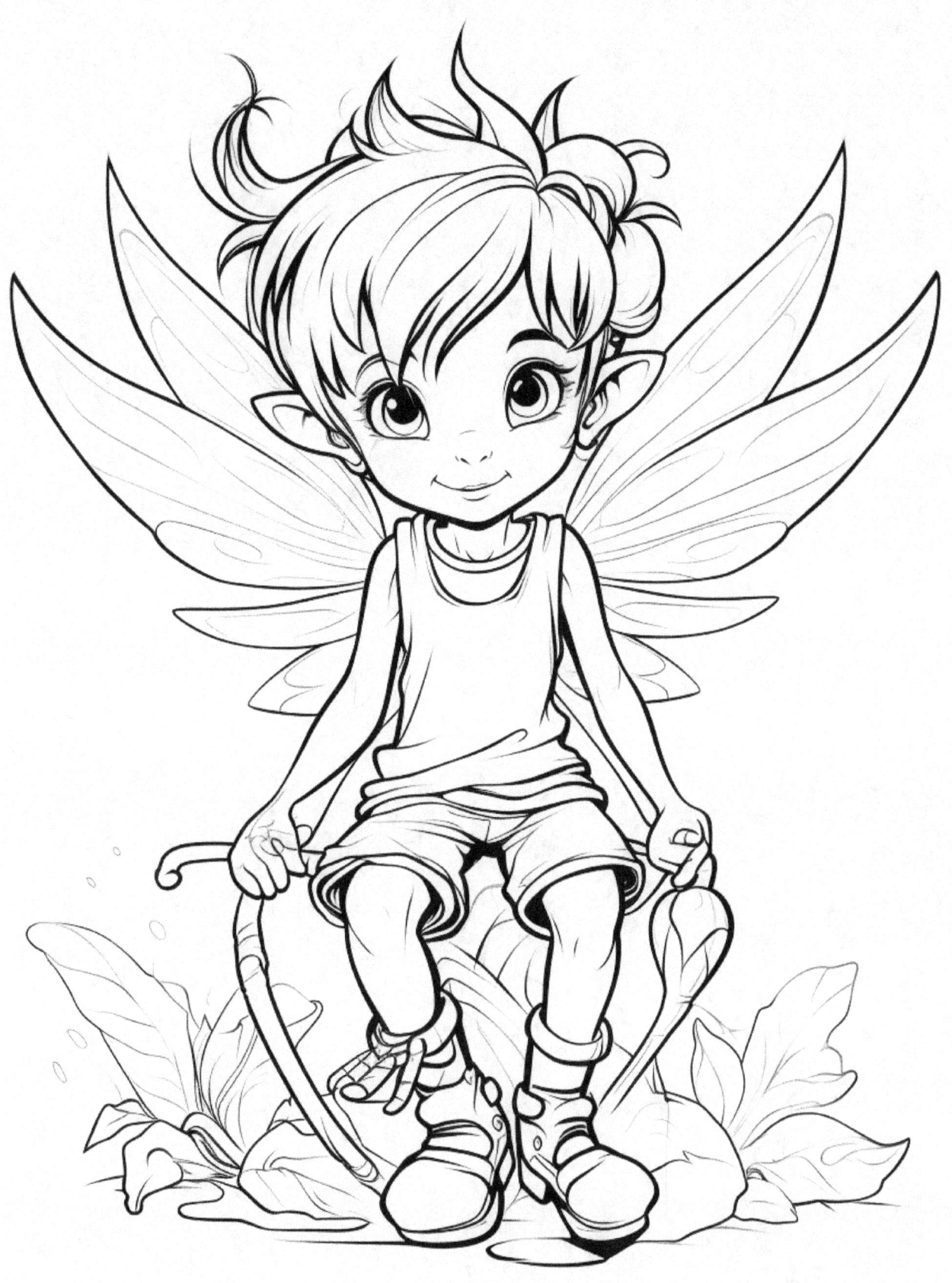

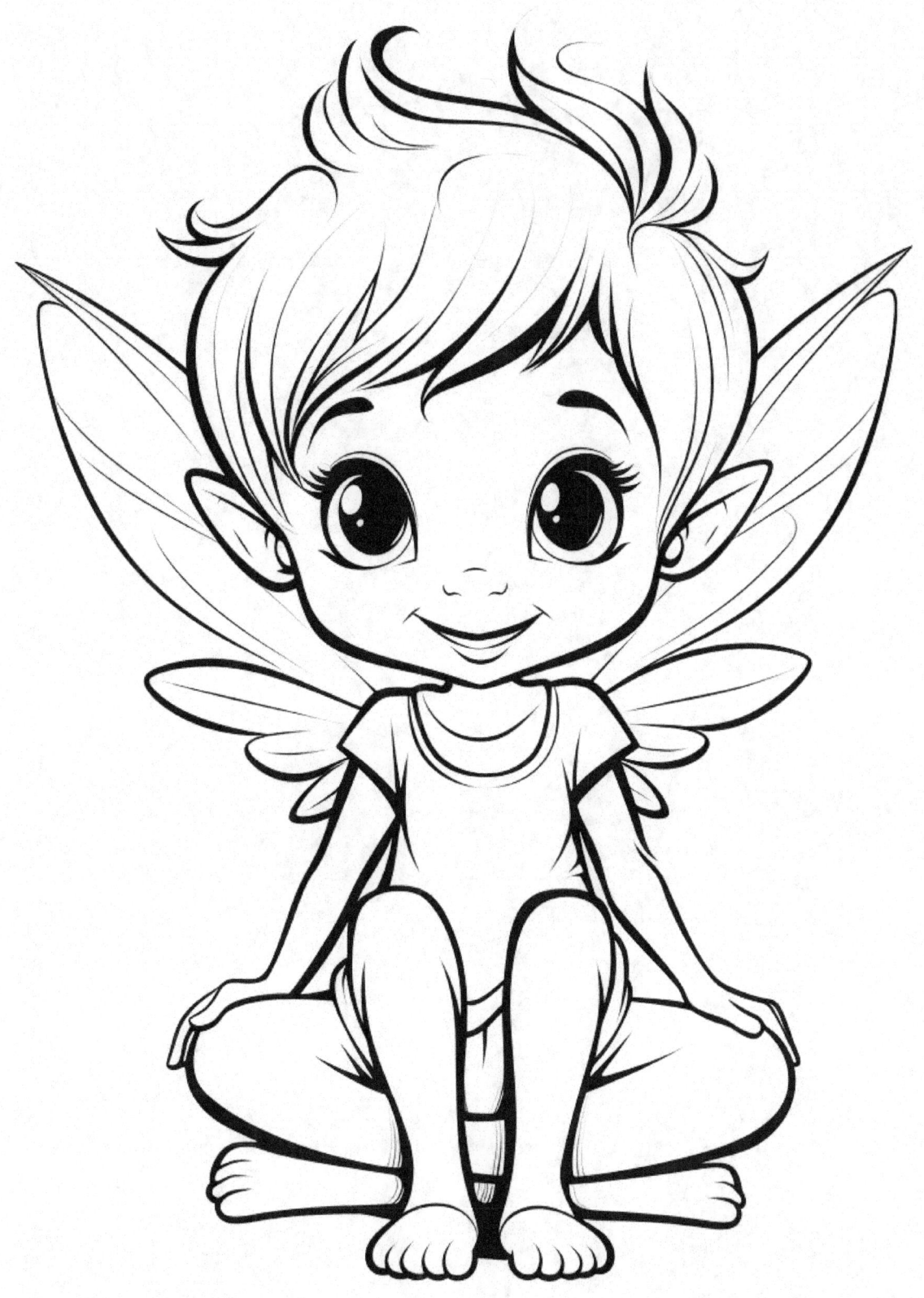

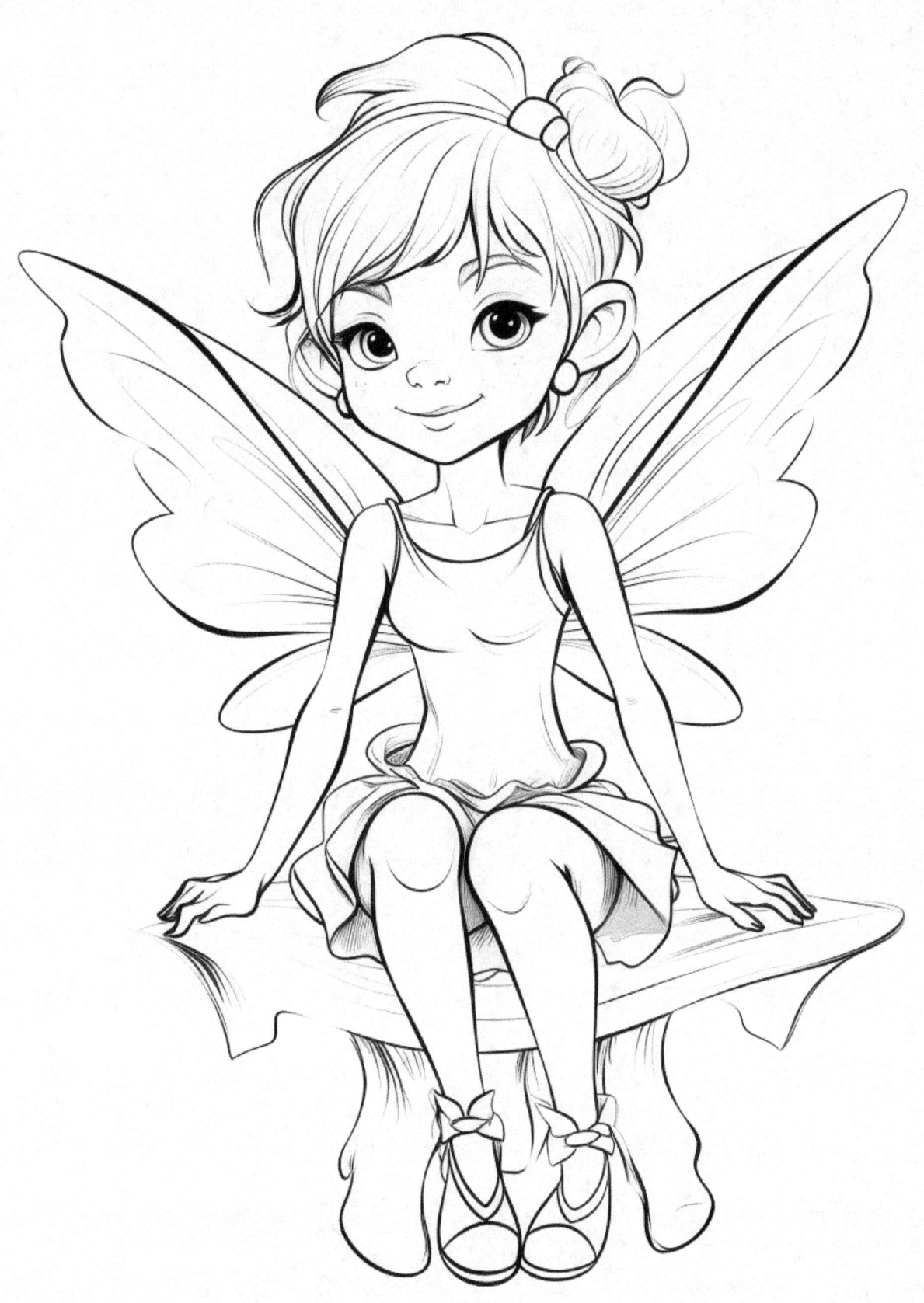

CYCLOPS

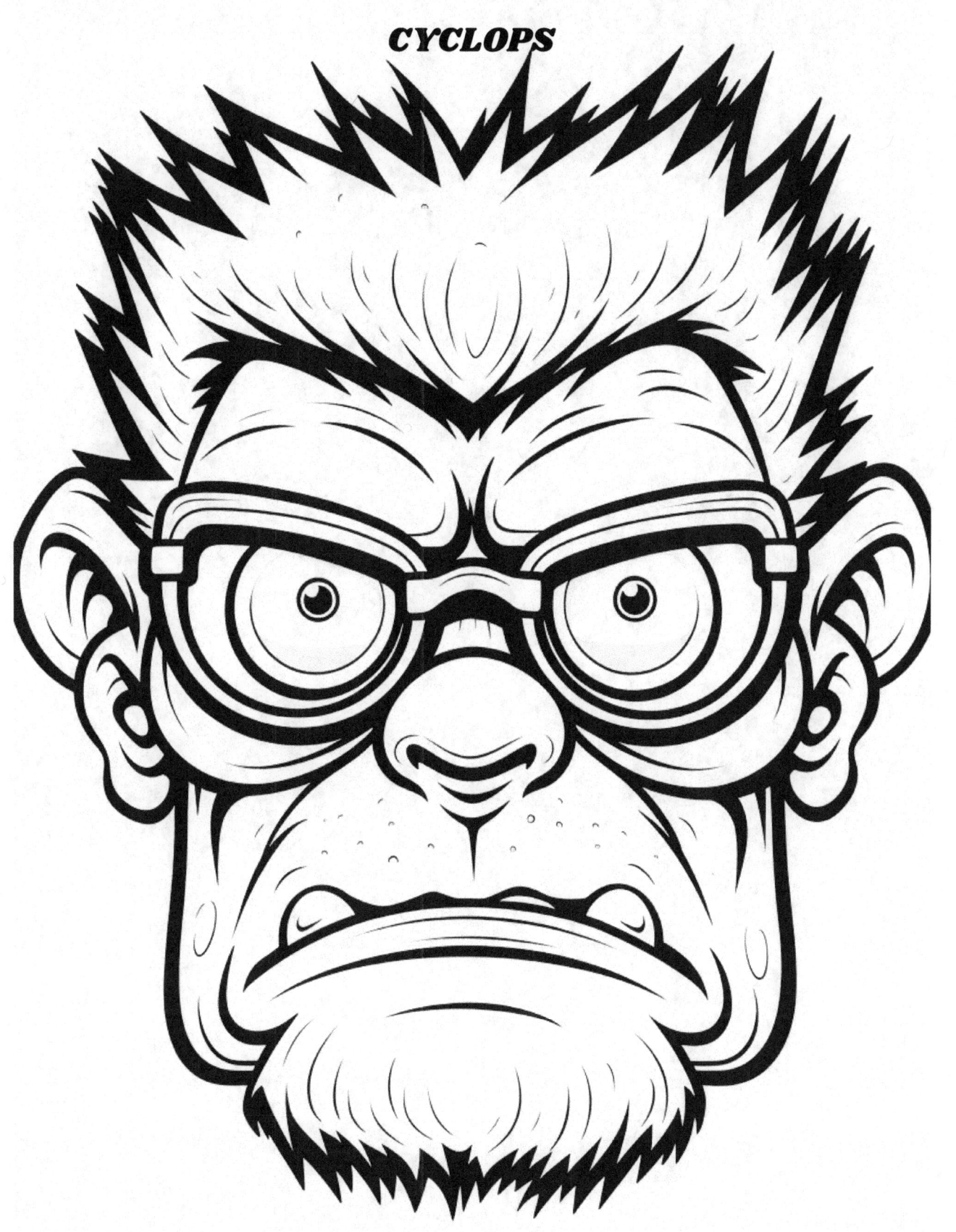

WYVERN

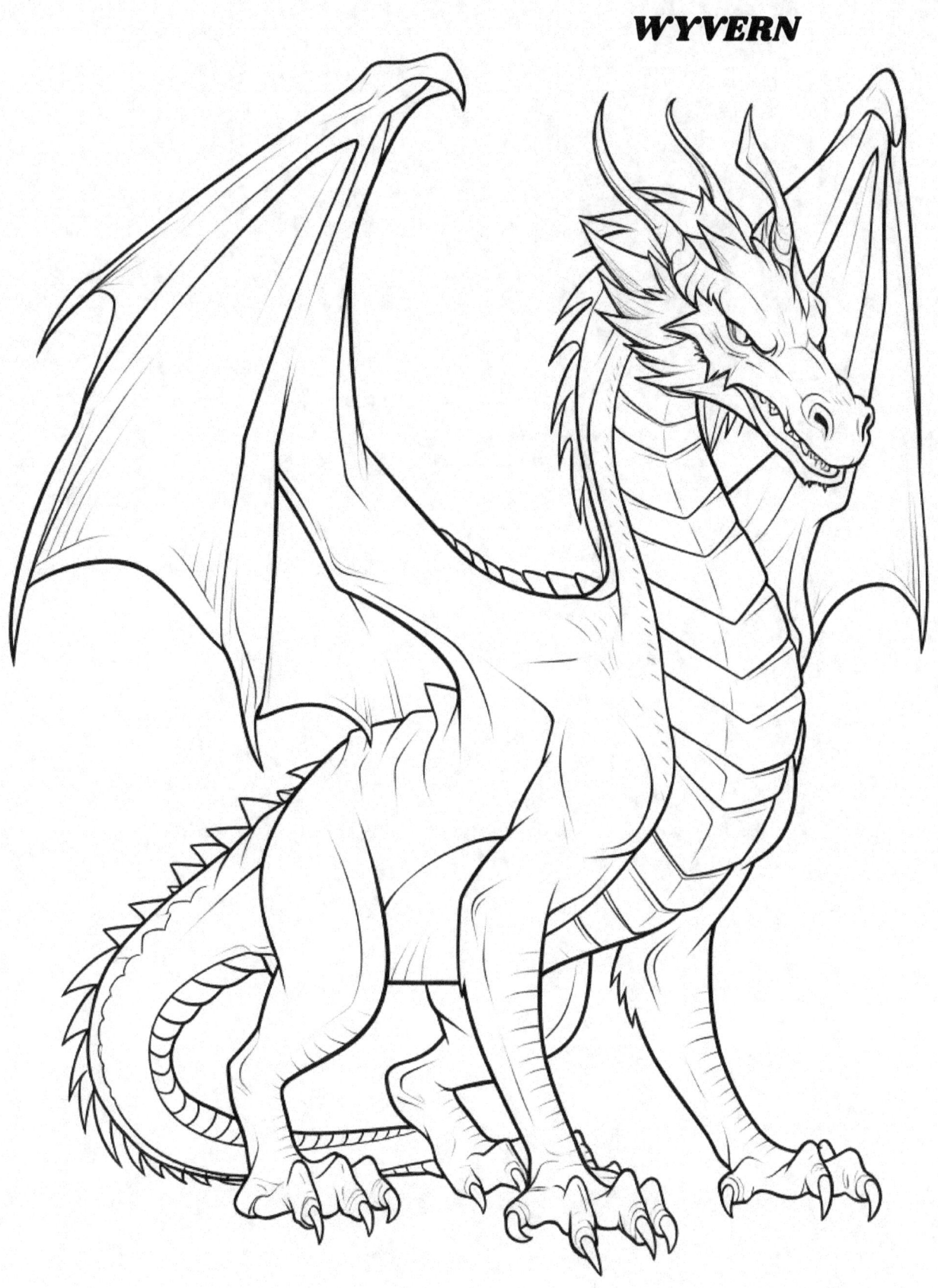

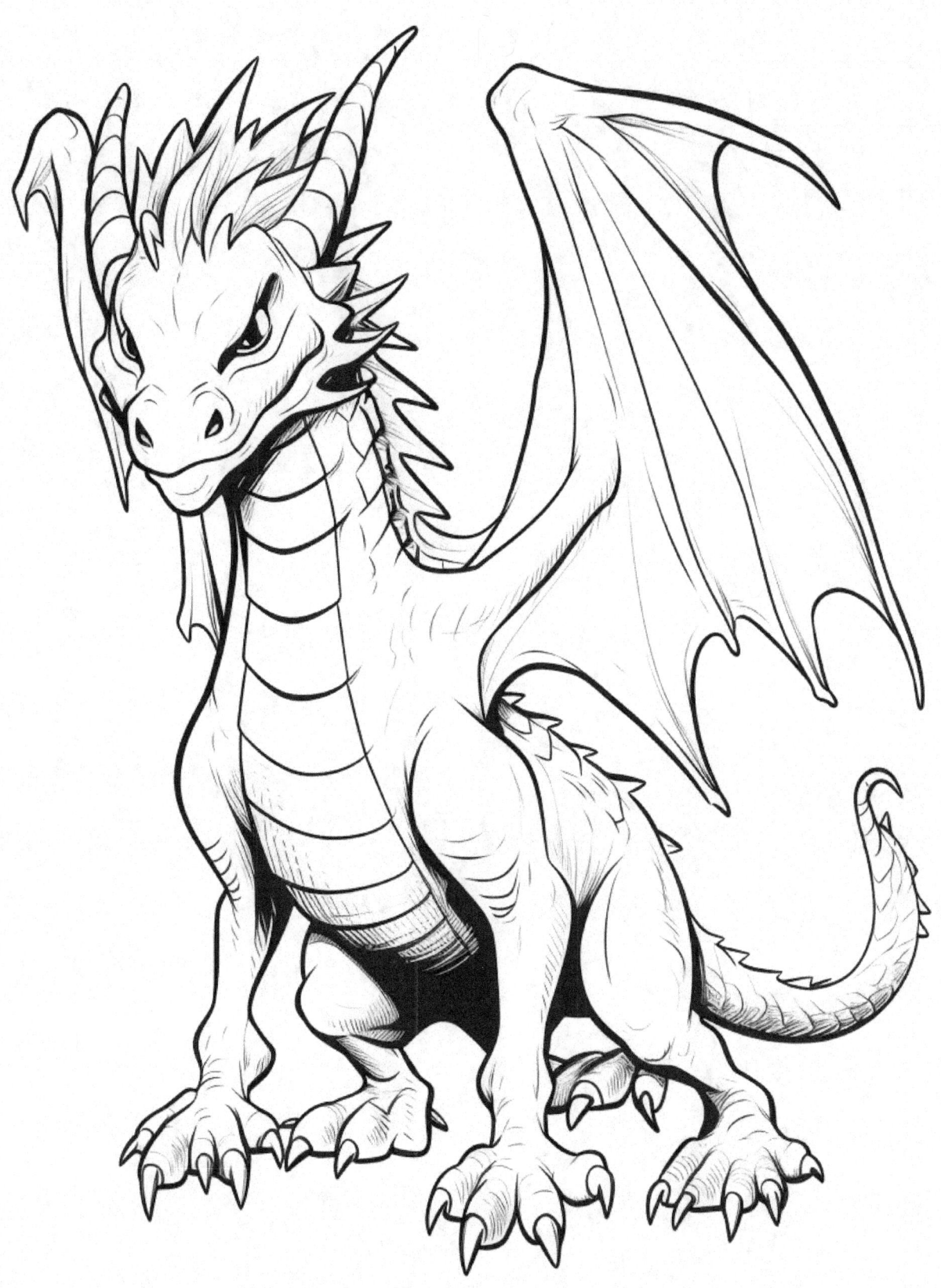